Mike – June 1982

May you have many
happy hours with your
rod & line.

Lin

PRACTICAL ANGLING
IN WORDS AND PICTURES

PRACTICAL ANGLING
IN WORDS AND PICTURES

Hans van Onck and Paul
Melief

with more than 200 illustrations

LUTTERWORTH PRESS
GUILDFORD AND LONDON

Photographs: Paul Melief and David Steuart
Sketches: Cor van Beurden
Translation: Marian Powell

ISBN 0 7188 2302 8

Printed in Great Britain
by Butler & Tanner Ltd, Frome and London

CONTENTS

Bags — Seat boxes and baskets — Tackle box — Angler's Table — Ground-bait tray or bucket — Bait droppers — Potato corer — Knives — Scissors and oddments — Pike disgorger and gag — Disgorgers — Bite indicators, bobbins, swing-tips and quivertips — Rod rests — Nets — Aeration pump — Livebait bucket — Leger leads — Bubble floats — Special keepnet holder

INTRODUCTION

Why do we fish?

Every angler must have asked himself this question at one time or another. Although the answer will vary from one person to another, some motives undoubtedly apply to all of us.

Each of us seeks excitement as well as recreation, and this is what angling supplies: it is an unequalled combination of sport and relaxation. It cannot be denied that an exciting fishing expedition in the company of like-minded friends, not lacking a certain measure of rivalry, releases us from our everyday cares and gives us a sense of happiness.

To let you share in this experience, while at the same time indicating the way to achieve the best results, is one of the main purposes of this book.

Does luck play a part?

We all know that there are anglers who appear to have 'golden hands', just as some gardeners have 'green fingers'. I am convinced that this is not purely a matter of luck, although in angling as in any other field there is always an element of chance. Let us consider the various factors involved. To begin with, the 'lucky' angler is always the one who perseveres. He carries on long after others have given up in despair because the fish won't bite. Nor does he readily move to another spot when, after initial good results, the fish cease to bite. He waits patiently for quite a time, every now and then varying his bait and the depths at which he fishes.

Thirdly, he refuses to accept failure. If he catches little or nothing he will not give up before having tried all possible variations in method.

And, finally, he is not one of those who set out from home declaring pessimistically that little result can be expected, because the weather conditions are all wrong. On the contrary, he knows that – happily – fish are so unpredictable that they may be caught in the worst, and remain absent in the most favourable, weather conditions.

To summarise: a 'lucky' angler possesses optimism, powers of perseverance, a comprehensive knowledge of angling and of fish, and efficient and varied equipment and bait.

Part 1

FRESHWATER

TECHNIQUE AND TACKLE

The general purpose rod

Like most things in life, angling is subject to fashion. When glass rods first appeared on the scene about twenty years ago, the majority of anglers, conservative fellows that they are, decided that it was not for them. Their beloved split-cane, craftsman-built quality rods, or whole Tonkin cane with just a top section of split-cane, could not be bettered they said. Good tubular glass fibre for general fishing has been proved better, however, and if one ex-amines in the tackle shop row upon row of general-purpose rods, specialist coarse-fishing rods, sea rods, game-fishing rods and the majority of fly rods, not one split-cane rod will be seen. 'Hollow glass' now dominates rod building materials.

The exceptions are some fly-rod designs that work better when made of split-cane, and a few fly and spinning rods of split-cane, produced at very high prices for a limited number of 'die-hards'.

Carbon fibre, the newest material to be used in the manufacture of fishing rods, is mostly confined to fly rod patterns. It is very expensive, and is therefore not likely to be used for general rod manufacture for some years. As an example, a little carbon

fibre fly rod will cost upwards of £60.00, and specialist coarse rods can run into hundreds of pounds. A good general-purpose coarse-fishing rod may be purchased in hollow glass for between £12.00 and £20.00, and for the very best of models between £30.00 and £45.00 at the time of publication of this book.

The best length for a general purpose rod would be 12 foot or 13 foot. Young men, or men of small stature, might find a 12 foot model a little easier to handle than a '13 footer', although, in truth, hollow glass rods are so light in comparison to the rods I used when a lad that most anglers should be able to manage the longer model and benefit from its advantages. The longer rod will make it easier fishing from rivers bordered with plants such as lilies or bankside rushes; it will help to fish deeper water with float tackle, and enable one to hold the long length of line between float and hook off the ground when casting; it will also help to play fish by steering them away from snags, especially bankside snags like fallen trees, or branches jutting into the water.

Photo 1. General purpose rods — all under £20.00.

Photo 2. General-purpose and match rods — over £20.00.

Photo 3. Poles. Used mostly on the Continent and by match anglers.

Photo 4. Floats mainly for river use.

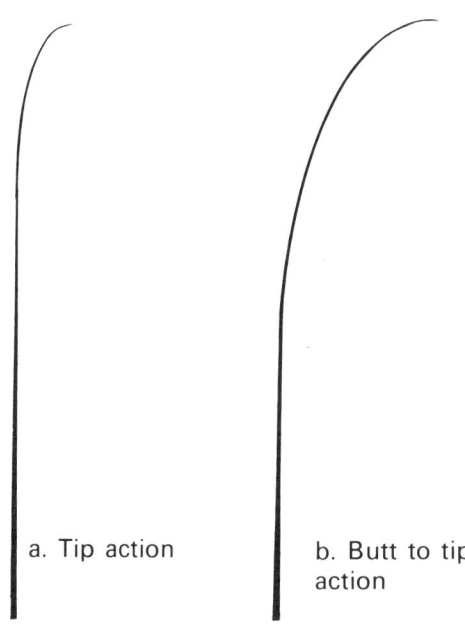

a. Tip action

b. Butt to tip action

Action

For general fishing, a rod with a bending action that operates nearly throughout its length is preferable as it can then be used for many purposes. (See sketch b on left.) It will handle fish of reasonable proportions, while still giving plenty of sport with the small ones.

Floats, plummets and shots

There are hundreds of patterns of floats and it would take a whole book to describe their uses. On account of their bright colours and great variety of shapes, it is tempting for all but the most self-disciplined angler to buy far more than he will ever use. I would suggest you ask your fishing tackle dealer for those most commonly used locally, and, if you are a novice insist that he shows you how to assemble the rod. This includes loading the reel with line, showing you how the float is placed on the line, and how to stabilise the line with shot according to the prevailing water conditions. You will also need to know how to attach and use a plummet to find the depth of the river or lake. If he refuses, take your custom elsewhere.

When it comes to buying lead shot, make sure that it is not too hard (you should be able to bite it easily between your teeth), otherwise it can damage the line. You will probably soon need a range of sizes from large to very small.

Photo 5. Assorted floats mainly used in still waters.
Photo 6. Various types of shot dispensers. Soft lead shot can be pressed on to the line by hand.
Photo 7. Lead plummets.
Photo 8. Method of attaching a standard plummet.

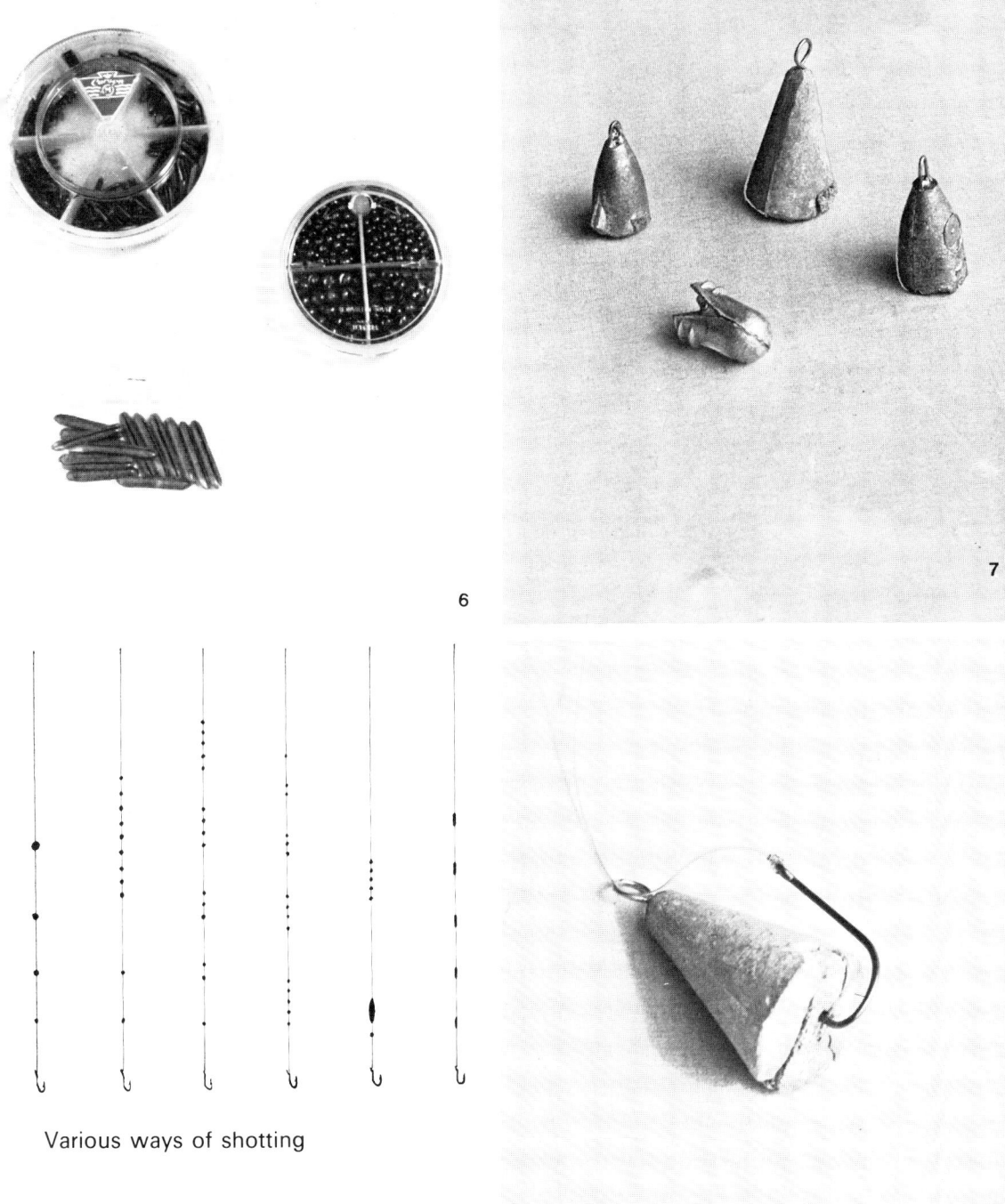

6

7

Various ways of shotting

8

Specialist rods

This subject can only be dealt with briefly as there are dozens of different types of rods, all made for different purposes. There are fly rods, spinning rods, carp rods, pike rods, sea rods of several sorts (dealt with in a separate chapter), telescopic rods, roach poles, legering rods, swing-tip and quiver-tip rods, swim-feeder rods, etc. Suffice it to say that the general purpose rod recommended will adequately serve for many of the techniques for which specialist rods are manufactured, although the angler who becomes proficient in any one of the many branches of angling may well decide he needs one of the special rods made for that particular purpose.

For fly fishing, and for fishing for the heavier species, like large carp and large pike, special rods will be necessary. Apart from fly fishing, though, the general-purpose rod will competently deal with small carp and pike, and a skilful angler may well land the occasional big fish hooked. The skilful angler would not use a general purpose rod for catching large fish by choice, but big fish do get hooked when fishing for smaller species or smaller sizes of a particularly large species.

Photo 1. Special rods, from left to right.
Spinning rod. There are several lengths and actions of spinning rods but not nearly so many as for fly rods. Nevertheless a beginner will still need advice when buying a spinning rod, although generally one can say that British-made rods of 6 or 7 feet are of light action (suitable for perch, small/medium pike, chub, or trout) and

those of 8–9 feet of medium action for medium to large pike, small to medium salmon, and large lake trout. Lengths of 10 feet or more usually apply to the strong rods for heavy salmon, or large pike.

Fly rod. There are many different lengths and actions of fly rod, whole books having been written on the subject. Never buy a fly rod from a tackle dealer who doesn't know anything about the particular kind of fly fishing you wish to do.

Pike rod. What is written below for carp rods will apply equally to pike rods. In fact, for some situations one can double for the other, and also for spinning.

Carp rod. There are two basic lengths of carp rods, the standard 10-foot and the 11-foot models for long casting and striking at distance. There are also extra strong models for big fish in waters with hidden obstacles.

Photo 2.

Telescopic rods. Shakespeare Ltd. produce several good models at reasonable prices, suitable for anglers who travel around on business and wish to have an easily transportable rod.

Photo 3.

Spigot joint. This form of rod joint is now the most popular and best means of joining together tubular glass sections.

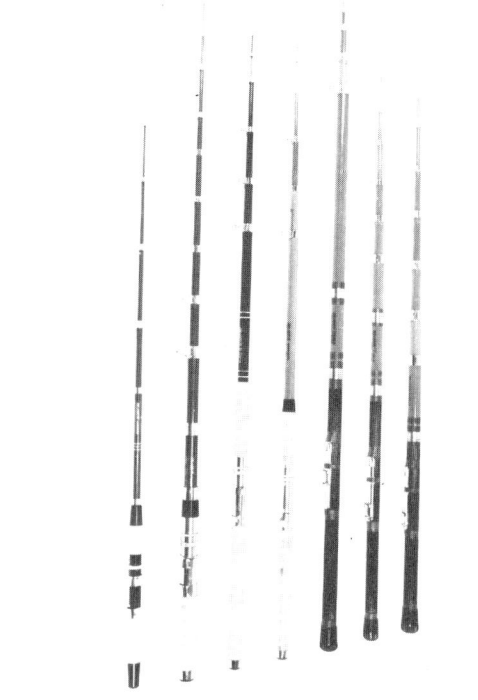

2

3

Reels

It appears that many anglers find it difficult to choose a suitable reel. Here, equally as when purchasing a rod, or any other equipment, my advice to the novice is to go to a reputable dealer who knows what angling is all about.

Nevertheless, he cannot advise you unless he knows for what purpose you intend to use the reel. Clearly, if it is only to serve for light fishing, or catching small fish, the demands made on the reel will be far less than when fishing for large fighting fish, i.e. game fish, large carp or pike. When should a reel be considered expensive, and when is it cheap? Of *all* equipment, it may be said that the cheapest may prove to be expensive if it is of poor quality, and the most expensive is cheap provided it is durable and efficient.

Good quality reels are made in Britain, France, and Scandinavia. Some of the finest multiplying reels in the world are Swedish made. Very expensive, but of wonderful quality and design!

So far as Japanese tackle is concerned, the manufacturers have long since realised that to retain their place in the world market, the quality as well as price must be competitive. This, of course, implies that Japanese reels are now no longer very cheap.

The modern angler is in any case sufficiently discriminating not to be foisted off with rubbish.

Wherever possible use a reel suited to your rod, that is, do not use a heavy reel with a light-weight rod and vice-versa.

The following are some popular reels of excellent designs. The manufacturers make other models of various sizes and prices.

Photo 4. *Mitchell 300*. The most popular French reel, used by thousands of anglers. Quick-change spools, perfect level winding design, and very smooth clutch.

Photo 5. *A.B.U. Cardinal 44*. This Swedish model of excellent quality uses *2* bale arm springs, the bale arm can be folded away to facilitate packing and to ease bale spring tension, and it also has quick change spools, good level winding, and a very smooth clutch.

Photo 6. *Intrepid New De-Luxe*. Very much cheaper than the previous two models, but this British made reel is still a very serviceable tool at the price. Spare parts, as with the expensive models, are readily obtainable.

Photo 7. *Daiwa*. A fairly high-priced Japanese reel of good quality.

Photos 8 and 9. A multiplier too can be very useful on a casting rod, especially when spinning or fishing with live bait. A rod with offset grip is often (though not necessarily) used. Braided nylon is nice to use with a multiplying reel, but modern monofilament nylon, even in heavy breaking strains, is reasonably supple and can be used satisfactorily nowadays. No nylon is entirely tangle free, but the supple types can be more easily knotted.

One-handed casting

Photo 10. The line is caught on the index finger before casting.
Photo 11. Overhead casting. (See also sketches on pp. 19–20.)

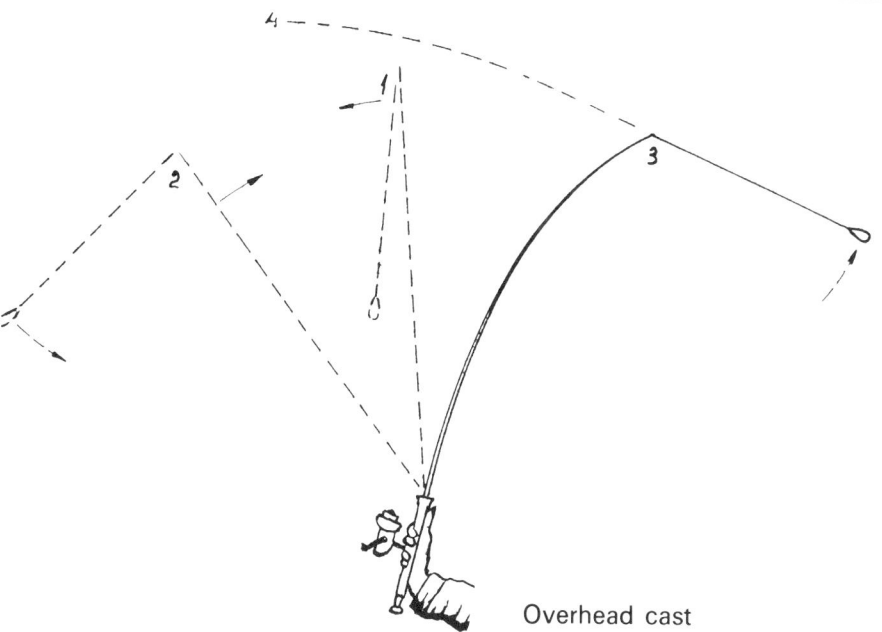

Overhead cast

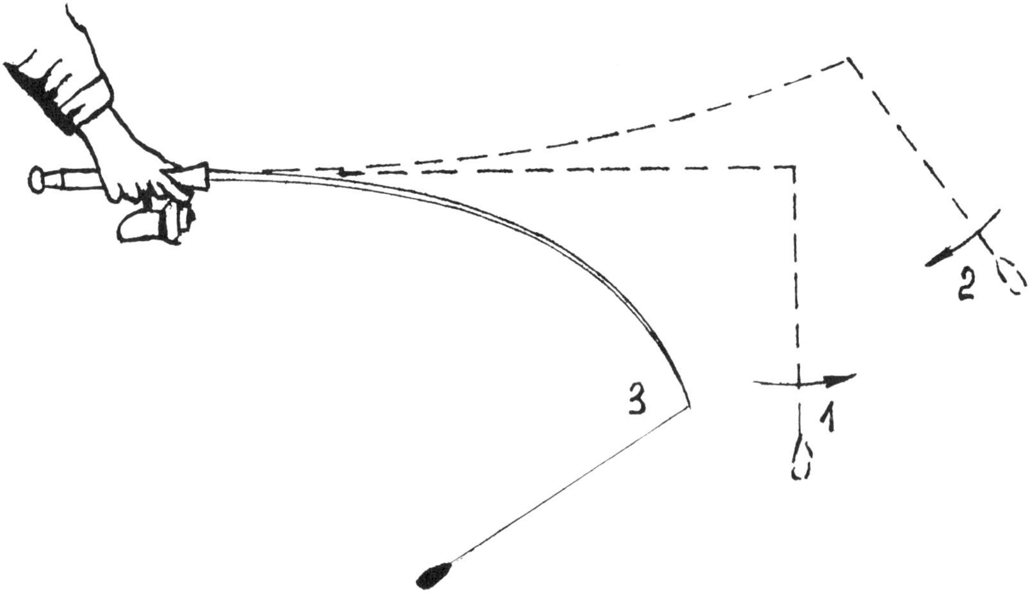

Sideways cast

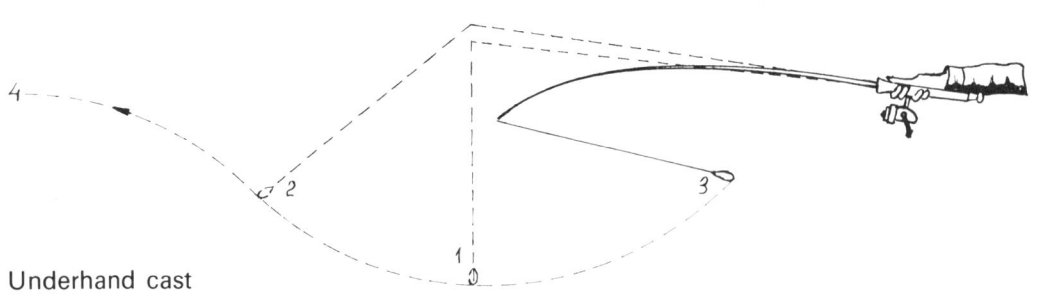

Underhand cast

Various aids

Photo 1. **Bags**

There is a large choice of holdalls on the market. They must fulfil a number of general requirements. To begin with, the bag must be made of a strong but supple material, and should preferably have two large compartments, two front pockets, two side pockets for the Thermos flask(s) and a rear pocket with a zip fastener for documents. Special flaps will keep the contents dry. Spools of line, tins of shot, hooks, etc., may be carried in one of the small front pockets, various small tools, such as hook extractors, scissors, etc., in the other. Handles and straps must be firmly attached, for they may have to carry a considerable weight. The bag in the photograph, by Shakespeare, has no side pockets, but it has the advantage that it may be carried either as a rucksack or by the grips – a great advantage to an active angler.

Photo 2. **Seat boxes and baskets**

Seat boxes, like the Efgeeco Company's 'Major Seat and Tackle Carrier', depicted in photograph 2, are far more popular in Southern England than the old fashioned basket. It is better anyway. It has a metal frame so is much stronger, it is waterproof, and besides keeping one's equipment dry, it will last much longer.

Photo 3. **Tackle box**

Increasing motor transport has resulted in another development: bigger and better tackle boxes are now being marketed. The one illustrated has three trays which lie parallel when the case is open so that all the contents can be seen at a glance. The bottom of the case provides space for larger pieces of equipment, such as reels, maggot and worm boxes, etc. If you buy such a case you should check carefully whether the hinges are sufficiently sturdy. In some makes they have extra strengthening.

Photo 4. **Tripod**

The bag in the photograph belongs to the author, not exactly the tidiest of fishermen. The purpose of the illustration is to show the tripod, which on many, many occasions has served to keep holdalls, jackets, rod-bags, etc., out of the mud. It consists of three bamboo sticks, available at low cost from any garden shop; these have been drilled at the top and are tied together with wire.

Photo 5. **Angler's table**

A folding table can be made easily that will fit into the tackle bag. Very useful for match anglers, for everything can be to hand. Various baits can be readily available, also disgorgers, shot, leger leads, change floats, scissors, anything that the matchman may consider will save time to have ready if needed. The table will also keep things tidy and easy for pleasure anglers. No need to bend down, no upset bait boxes, no time-consuming groping in the bag.

Photo 6. **Groundbait tray or bucket**

There are many types of ready-made bait on the market: most of them are excellent. Where the groundbait has to be mixed with water, this is best done with the water in which you intend to fish. A folding plastic bait tray, easily transported in the holdall, is very practical and avoids the necessity of carrying a bucket. Various types of bait are described in the section on bream (p. 48).

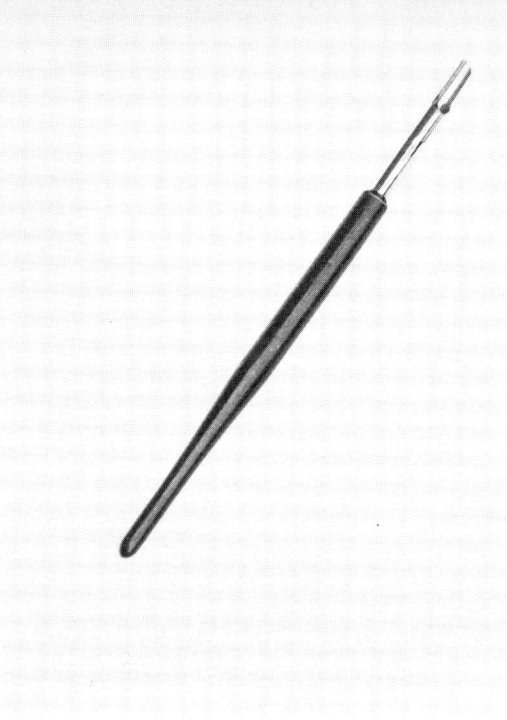

Photo 7. **Bait droppers**

Many amateur anglers encounter difficulties with ground baiting. Having carefully prepared the swim, they find that unforeseen circumstances cause the hook to settle away from the baited area. This may happen, for instance, where the angler is fishing from a boat riding on one anchor, or where wind and current plague the inexperienced fisherman. The 'Thamesley' bait dropper illustrated is attached to the hook and opens when it touches bottom. Swim-feeders (not illustrated) are legers containing groundbait. There are several on the market and all help considerably to bring success.

Photo 8. **Potato corers**

Many fish – carp, for instance – eagerly take boiled potato. A potato corer is useful for making small size baits. All one needs is a piece of tubing of the required diameter and a piece of dowel. The tube is pushed through the potato and the dowel pushes the potato from the tube. The *potato* dowel is then broken off to length. An even simpler device is an old-fashioned pen with the nib reversed as shown.

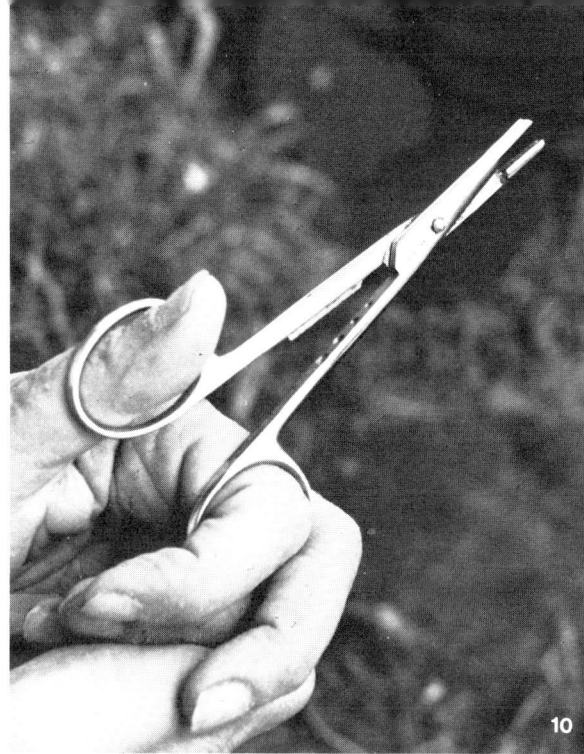

Photo 9. **Knives**

Every angler's equipment must include a good knife. This is not as simple as it sounds. There are knives on the market which at first sight appear to be ideal because of their numerous gadgets: small pliers, small scissors, a little file, etc. In practice these knives are useless. Take a simple, really rustproof knife with a fairly narrow blade and a reasonably heavy handle which can be used to knock fish on the head if required for eating.
The knife in the photograph has a cork handle and cannot sink.

Photo 10. **Scissors and oddments**

Although a knife serves several purposes, a pair of scissors is equally indispensable. Or rather, several pairs. To begin with, small scissors that may be carried in the pocket, in case your bag is some distance away. I have a small pair of scissors with curved points, which I find most satisfactory. In addition the combination scissors shown in photograph 10 are very useful, for they will cut hooks as well as nylon. A small pair of pliers should also lie to hand.

Photo 11. **Pike disgorger and gag**

The disgorger shown is suitable for removing hooks from pike; also in the picture is a gag for holding the pike's jaws apart while the 'operation' is performed. Dedicated pike anglers like to treat their catches with reverence so that they may be returned to the lake or river without any damage. The gag points are therefore removed with care. The disgorger shown is strong enough, and long enough, to keep the fingers away from those large, sharp teeth.

N.B. There is a special instrument for holding eels firmly while removing hooks, which is shown in photograph 3, p. 65.

Photos 12 and 13. **Disgorgers**

There are numerous types of disgorgers on the market, some a little easier to use than others, but none of them serviceable unless used correctly. Hold the fish in a wet hand, without squeezing it but sufficiently firmly to avoid dropping it if it wriggles, since this might damage the fish. Insert the disgorger along the line and push back the hook without causing further damage with the barb. The scissors in photograph 10 (p. 25) have a V-shaped notch at the tip and can be used as pliers if the hook is caught firmly. Photograph 13 shows it being used. Many anglers use surgical forceps for this purpose: not only are these

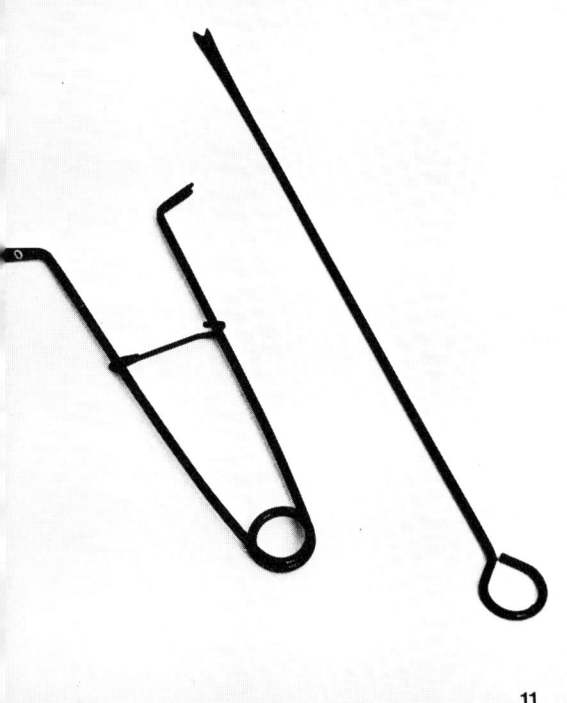

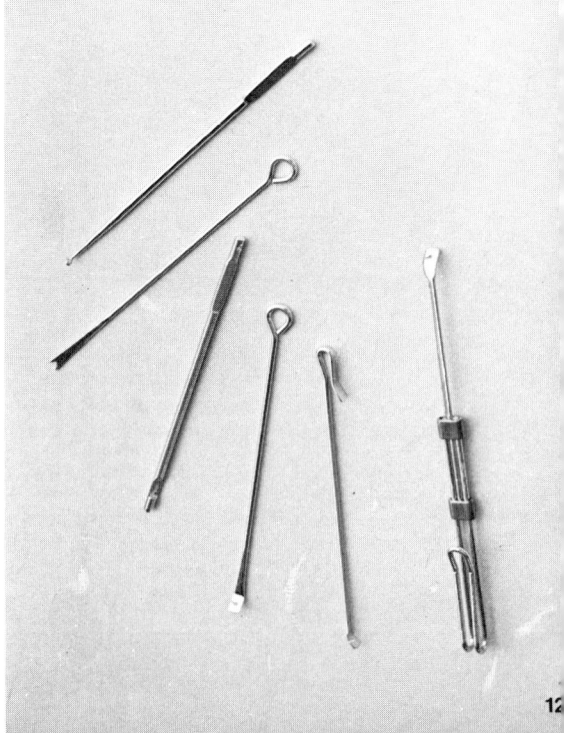

11

12

very effective: they are also perfectly rust-proof.

Photos 14, 15 and 16. **Bite indicators, bobbins, swing-tips and quiver-tips**

Bite indicators might justifiably be included in the section dealing with floats, for their function is about the same, i.e. to signal a bite. However, as you will read elsewhere in this book, the float serves other purposes as well, and it is for that reason that they are dealt with separately. Some of the bite indicators described here do not form an integral part of the tackle, but should be removed as soon as possible after the fish has been struck. Obviously

they are used only when angling without a float, with or without lead.

There are various methods of attaching an indicator. Often it is inserted between reel and butt ring, because this is the easiest place to attach it after casting and from which to remove it when playing a fish.

If the bottom of a bobbin is attached by a length of nylon to the base of the rod rest, it should pull free of the line without getting lost when striking a bite.

The simplest way of all is to fold a piece of silver paper over the line, but this will not work very well on a windy day unless shielded.

There are two attachments used by a majority of anglers when legering, the

15

swing-tip, shown in use in photograph 15, and the quiver-tip. These are screwed into a threaded tube in the rod's top ring. Most manufacturers incorporate these rod top rings in their general-purpose, match, and legering rods. The quiver-tip works as a sensitive rod tip extension, while the swing-tip works like a bobbin by hanging down and putting an angle in the line.

For night fishing the same bobbins can be used, and seen by shining a torch upon them. One can, however, purchase a bobbin with a 'light source' of tritium gas. Contained within a plastic tube it will glow for many years, ten years or more (photograph 16). Alternatively, for anglers who do not wish to watch something, for hours per-

haps when after big carp at night, audible types of bite detection devices are available. One of the best that has been in production for several years is the 'Heron' bite detector. This detector will show a light when a fish bites at the same time as it produces an audible buzz. The light serves a twofold purpose, as explained in the following paragraph.

Many anglers use two rods when carp fishing, and the flashing light will tell them which rod has the bite when the tackle cannot be seen in the dark, and one wishes to use the audible method of bite detection. It will also show one when the battery is low – act as a bit of insurance too – for if the power is insufficient to activate the

'buzzer', the light will work for quite a while, still giving a bite indication, though visual only.

Photo 17. The 'Heron' bite detector, consists of a rod rest top, with an antenna around which the line is passed, and a battery and buzzer box.
N.B. In sea fishing there are entirely different methods of signalling a bite. In freshwater fishing, too, there are other possibilities, without the use of a bite indicator. These will be mentioned separately in the descriptions of various angling methods.

Photo 18. **Rod rests**

Another subject about which many pages could be filled, for they exist in numerous types and sizes. Unfortunately, I have discovered few that are entirely satisfactory, for one needs different rod rests for different jobs. When carp or pike fishing, for example, one often requires a rod rest which will not trap the line but allow it to run freely through the rest (photograph 18). This type of rest will serve most purposes, but match anglers often prefer the wide rod tops that will screw into a bank stick. I don't really know why.
There is always the problem that the ground is too hard to push in the rod rest

19   20

21   22

and at times one may be fishing from a concrete platform or a wooden jetty. One firm, Efgeeco, manufactures a rod rest that will overcome these problems, and one or two others, e.g. the 'Adaptarest'.

It is usual to use a back-rest to keep the rod and reel completely clear of the ground for some forms of angling — carp or pike fishing again — and this manner of 'set-up' is also depicted in photograph 18. The reason is obvious. When a big fish is running out line at speed from a fixed spool reel, with the bale arm in the open position, it would be extremely foolish to allow the line to catch in terrestrial growth.

Photos 19–23. **Nets**

I am struck by the fact that nets, even when satisfactory in themselves, are frequently used incorrectly.

Photo 19. Various landing nets. (Never 'scoop' a fish!)
The centre net is used in trout fishing, when the fisherman is standing out in the water, wearing thigh boots or a fishing suit.

Photo 20. Landing net with a long, telescopic handle, often used in matches, but also very useful where there is a wide belt of weeds or reeds along the bank.

Photo 21. Ideal for the fly-fisher. The handle has a folding, not a sliding action and can be extended with one hand.

Photo 22. Keep nets are never ideal, not even if made of nylon. A knotless net is the most humane. If you do want to use a keep net, one with flexible rings is useful: the rings are made of polythene and the net can be folded to go into a tackle carrier. The bank stick of the keep net illustrated is long enough to be set next to the angler, who therefore need not get up to put the fish into it.

Photo 23 (page 32). Landing net in which the handle is extended automatically by pressing a button. This net is available in several sizes.

Photo 24. **Aeration pump**

A small aeration pump (Shakespeare) will keep livebait fresh and alive: it may be attached to any livebait bucket.

Photo 25. **Livebait bucket**

Only the *largest* plastic bucket manageable should be used for transporting livebait.

Photo 26. **Leger leads**

As can be seen there are many kinds of leads used for legering. Probably the most popular and therefore the most widely used is the Arlesey Bomb, which is the swivelled bomb-shaped lead in the top left-hand corner of the picture.

26

27

Photo 27. **Bubble floats**

These are celluloid bubbles which, partly or entirely filled with water, serve as casting weights and, if required, as floats. For easier observation the transparent bubble may be filled with milk or a coloured liquid by means of an eye dropper, via a hole which can be closed.

Photo 28. **Special keepnet holder**

Although the keepnet attachment shown for fixing to a boat's gunwale is not available in this country, one is easily made from a bank-stick and a clamp.

28

1

2

3

4

Fly fishing

Fly fishing is becoming more and more popular. Manufacturers and importers have quickly caught on and outfits can be bought for under £20.00. The time is past when fly fishing was thought to be a hobby for the rich and leisured classes only: something that could only be learnt by years of practice and even then would remain a difficult art. The former belief has, as was said above, been scotched to some extent: the latter may contain a grain of truth.

Fishing for trout or salmon in waters of which the banks are frequently overgrown may certainly be difficult, but in low-lying areas, where the banks are often clear, fly fishing – for instance for rudd – is a much simpler matter, even though the wind may present problems. I would advise you to practise before you actually start fishing.

Fortunately the modern tubular glass rods are not nearly as fragile (if, perhaps, in a few cases, not as good either) as the old split-cane rods. It is advisable to start with an inexpensive rod.

Should you wish to *specialise* someday in fly-fishing, there are many excellent books available on all aspects of the subject. Meanwhile this section will start you on your way, the photographs and sketches explaining the rudiments. If possible, start by fly fishing for coarse fish – rudd, dace, etc.

Photos 1, 2 and 3. Different grips in fly casting. The grip in photograph 1 avoids the beginner's mistake of taking the rod too far back when casting.

Photo 4. The left hand guides the line by pulling more from the reel each time the rod returns to a horizontal position.

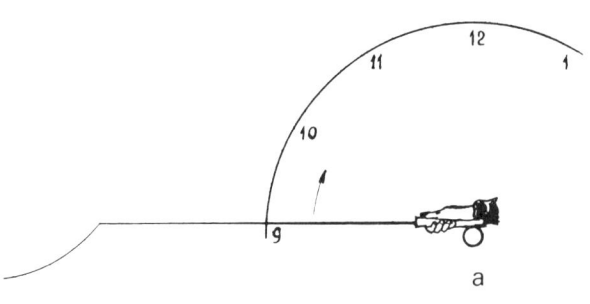

a

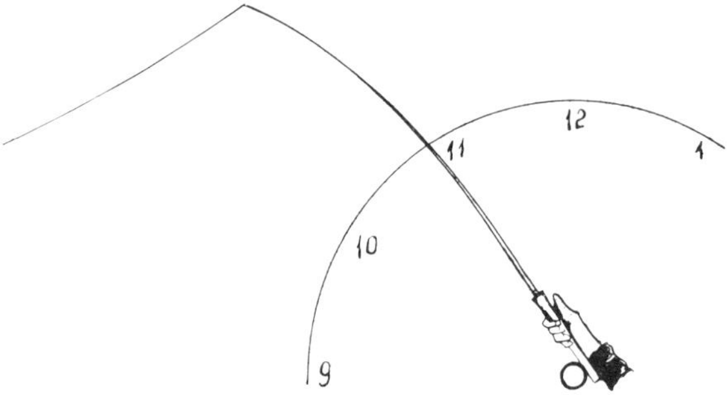

b

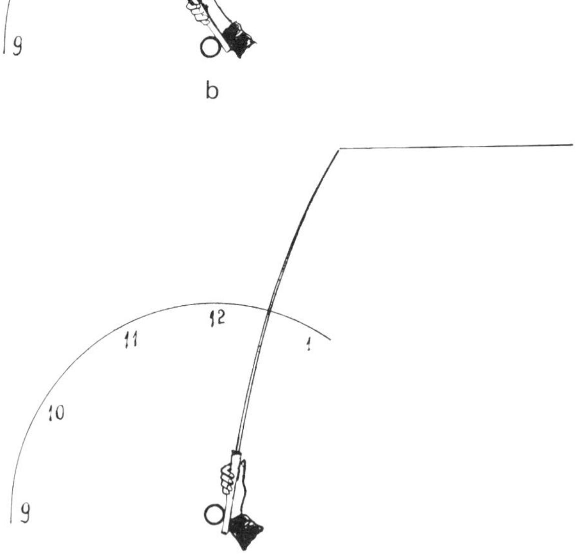

c

36

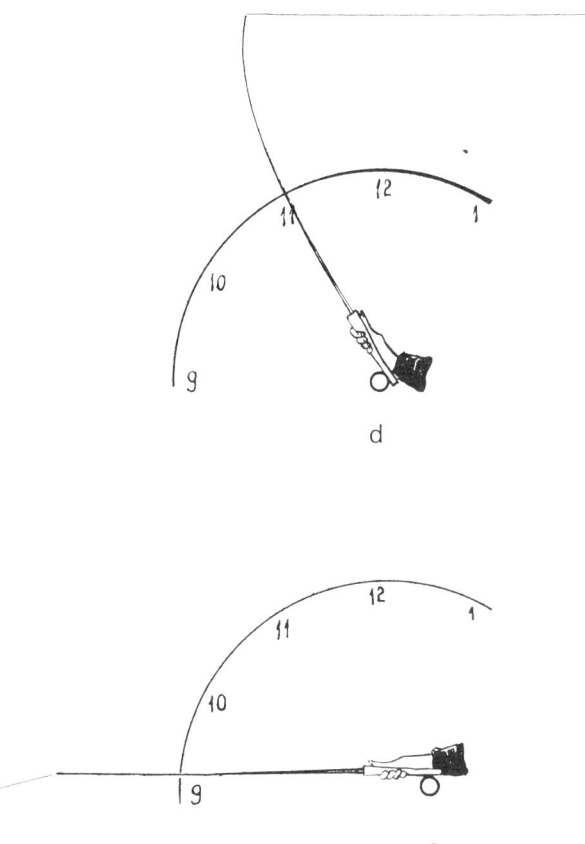

d

e

Sketches a–e. A right-handed cast from start to finish. The left hand holds the line tight between reel and rod and lengthens it by pulling more line from the reel each time the rod goes back. See photograph 4 (p. 34).

6

7

The photographs on p. 38 show how to use any available cover. This brings me to a point which needs special attention. All fish – certainly all big fish – are shy and as a rule this fact is overlooked. Waters in low-lying areas, such as illustrated, often hold rudd of 10 inches and more. Walking quietly along the banks, or taking the trouble to watch for a while, you will see the V-shaped furrows made by the big boys. Now walk along carelessly and I bet that you will see the fish racing off as far away as eight or ten yards. They are sensitive to the sound vibrations transmitted over this distance by the soggy ground.

Avoid white caps or other bright clothing. Also avoid your shadow falling over the water, especially where the water is shallow. There are still too many anglers with shiny ferrules on their rods. Get rid of the shine, or paint them black.

Photos 5, 6 and 7. An experienced fly fisher will stay as far away from the bank as possible, and will preferably crouch or kneel.

Photos 8 and 9. The fish has taken the fly and been hooked. When playing the fish the line is pressed against the rod with the right hand and 'stripped' in with the left.

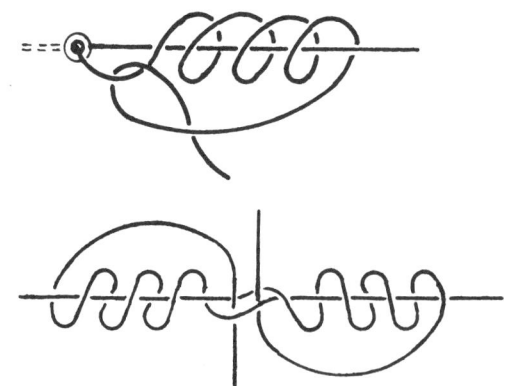

To many anglers the selection of flies presents a problem. The choice is enormous, but don't let it worry you. Buy a few good dry flies (for instance, dressed Palmer fashion) in two colours and in two or three different sizes, from a knowledgeable dealer. Try them out in the waters where you fish most often.

Photo 10. *Dry* fly, i.e. one that floats.
Photo 11. *Wet* fly. This is presented to the fish under water, with short jerks on the line, or a steady draw.

Above: Attaching a line to an eyelet
Below: The correct method of joining two lines

Photo 12. A good simple fly reel. The reels serve only for running off and retrieving line. There are automatic reels on the market as well: these may be more convenient, for instance, where the angler has to move through long grass, but they have the disadvantage of being fairly heavy.

Photo 13. A fine rudd in play. For rudd fishing, see pp. 44–7.

Photo 14. An artificial fly is nearly always attached at the front of the mouth, enabling it to be removed without damaging the fish. Note the upward slant of the rudd's mouth, which indicates a surface feeder.

THE FISH

Roach

In this country the roach (*Rutilus rutilus*) is probably the fish most often caught. It is not a difficult fish to catch — not the little ones at any rate, for they are nearly always willing to bite, and can, in fact, be quite a nuisance. Larger specimens, generally, stay close to the bottom and the favourite method of fishing for them is by float fishing, but catches of very big roach are often made by anglers who specialise in legering techniques to fish for them a long way out in large lakes and reservoirs.

Chalk stream type rivers, and clear canals rich with weed, will also grow roach to specimen proportions.

Usually small baits and small hooks are used but at times it will take large baits, or any common baits. In many places it is caught with hemp. A little known, but excellent bait is provided by the long threads of weed found on stones and posts. Run the hook through it, twisting it until you have a little plug of weed round the shank. The point of the hook need not be hidden. In late autumn and in winter roach seek the deepest water, where you may take fine catches. Like all fish, roach at that time of the year is less hungry and prefers soft bait, for instance very soft

paste, or better, flake. (*Photograph 1, p. 45.*) Nevertheless these fish will take maggot in winter, and during or after floods, worms are a very good bait.

As a rule the roach is a fighter and will give us plenty of sport when it resists arrest.

The smaller specimens are plentiful in most fishing waters, and not too difficult to catch with the lightest tackle. Larger ones are scarce. If your roach weighs over a pound you have really cornered a worthy opponent!

The photographs speak for themselves.

Photo 1. Fishing for winter roach in the River Kennet.

Photo 2. A nice roach from the Dorset Stour.

Photo 3. A sizeable roach has almost given up the struggle;

Photo 4. it is being carefully unhooked (bait: maggot) before being returned to 'the bosom of its family'.

Rudd

Rudd (*Scardinius erythrophthalmus*) is found in waters all over the country, especially where reeds and waterplants grow. It is a fine, sporting fish, not too difficult to catch. Its mouth, slanting upwards, indicates that it is a surface feeder, but large specimens may be caught close to the bottom, especially in large stretches of water. It will eat anything and is, in fact, a veritable bandit (although not officially classified among predatory fish). I have caught it more than once when spinning for quite different 'game', as, for example, when using a fairly large bar-spoon. No doubt this fish takes smaller specimens of its own kind.

For this fish we use practically the same method as for roach, except that we fish higher in the water, often, in fact, just below the surface.

However, its mode of life enables us to waylay the fish in quite different ways as well, one of the nicest being fly-fishing. (For the technique of casting and fly-fishing, see pp. 34–41.) The pleasant thing about this method is that waters may be fished which are practically inaccessible for other forms of angling: clear, shallow waters with overgrown banks. In such circumstances we cautiously creep along, preferably at some distance from the bank. With a bottom rod one fishes far off. A small float, about 4 in. above the hook, a single shot and a hook size to suit the bait. For bait: bread, flake, maggot, worms — anything will do. The bait is dropped gently, close to weeds or lily pads — the float dips and the rudd immediately 'hangs'

itself. Success is also likely when fishing from a boat which is gently pulled alongside an overgrown bank. (I have in this way often had surprises with quite different and larger types of fish.) A light spinning rod, a weighted float and the same single shot as described above will give even better sport. Many amateur fishermen prefer to ambush the rudd by means of only the lightest of spinning rods with tiny barspoons, with or without a fly. However, in long weeds this is not much fun.

One of the most pleasant ways to fish is undoubtedly with spinning rod and weighted float along reed fringed pools and lakes, as in the following photographs of a fishing expedition:

Photo 1. This is 'flake'. A piece of *fresh* white bread is pressed around the hook. Another bread bait is soft paste. This is best made from stale bread (not mouldy) to which water is added, then kneaded between the hands until it is of a suitable consistency. It must be soft enough to strike the hook through, but feel dry to the touch.

Photo 2. Weighted float and shotting. The shot lies close to the float, so that bait and hook drop lightly.

Photo 3. The angler has picked a good spot (the wind on his back) at about 15 yards from the reeds. The stakes have been placed as quietly as possible.

N.B. If possible pick a strip of reeds with a narrow channel of open water behind it for this method.

Photo 4. Cast in such a way that float and bait lie *very* close to the reeds: as little as 4 inches may make all the difference. If the wind is in the right direction, the gear will in any case float towards the reeds.

Photo 5. The bait lies in the correct spot — it will probably not be there for long, for any rudd present will take it immediately, provided the time of day is right, that is, very early in the morning twilight, and especially just before it gets dark.

Photos 6, 7 and 8. These photographs speak for themselves. A finer fish than the rudd would be difficult to find.

One further remark: using this method it is inevitable that the hook will sometimes get caught in the reeds. When this happens break the line with a sharp tug and recover a lost float at a later stage, for if you row to the bank straight away, you will find that the fish have departed. It is therefore advisable always to have a number of 'spares' to hand.

This then, is one — and for the average angler, perhaps the most attractive — method, but if you have read the chapter on fly-fishing with proper attention, you will realise that the rudd will gladly take a fly, provided it is presented correctly. Odd things may happen in this connection: the following is a good example. A group of knowledgeable fly-fishermen had arranged a friendly match in a lake, with pitiful results. A few small rudd took the fly, or merely mauled the hackles, so that after a short time the fly became unusable. There was, however, an exception. One of the anglers landed fine fish one after another. How was this possible? When finally he landed the biggest rudd I have ever seen (15 inches) it became too much for the rest of us. Swallowing our pride, we went to find out how it was done. It proved to be

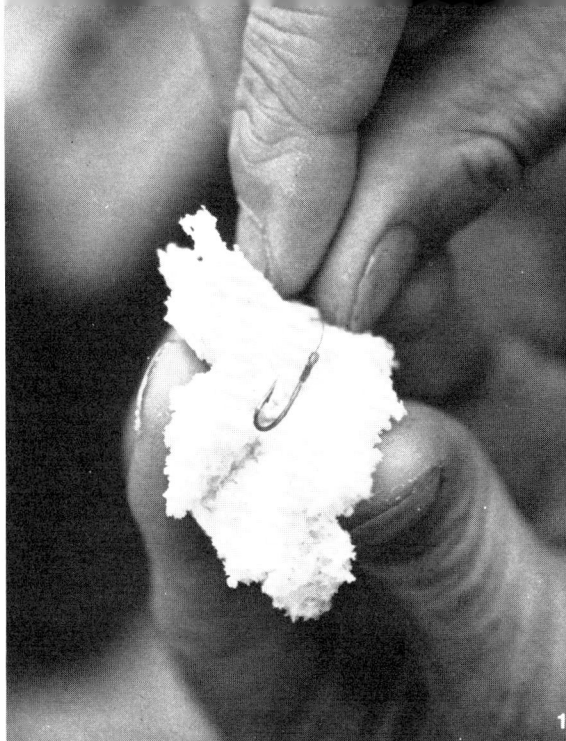

quite simple: the successful angler was using an ordinary black fly, like the rest of us, but his had a red tag and it was this that had done the trick. When we did the same, our catches improved considerably. The most surprising thing is that, although on later occasions I frequently used the same fly in that particular lake, it never took any more rudd than other flies.

Bream

It seems probable that in some areas more anglers fish for bream than for any other fish, where it occurs in such large numbers that it is usually easily caught, and it is, moreover, large enough to make quite a show. It is true that some anglers rather despise *Abramis brama*, calling it slimy and sluggish – the former with justice, the latter not. I, too, prefer to get rid of this slab-sided fish as quickly as possible, and when fishing from a boat I try to unhook it without bringing it aboard. Nevertheless, like many hundreds of thousands of anglers, I enjoy fishing for bream, and I therefore feel justified in devoting a fair amount of space

to this fish. To ignore it would be a case of misplaced snobbery.

Bream is a fish which likes a quiet life. Photo 1 above shows a typical bream-fisher, as he may be found everywhere. All his equipment is to hand, so that he rarely needs to get up. He has prepared a good swim, close to the lily pads on the opposite side of the water, and this is where his bait is lying, over a substantial quantity of groundbait – essential for a big catch. As for bait, whenever possible I prefer bread, either flake or paste (see under 'Rudd', p. 44), photograph 1 (p. 45), but bream are also fond of maggots and small dung-worms.

Photo 2. Box of maggots. Like all bait, they

should be kept as cool as possible. Be sure to keep the box securely closed when you are at home, for they are quite capable of opening the lid and then you'd be in trouble. Tape down the lid on both sides with Sellotape.

Photo 3. This, in my opinion, is the correct way to hook maggots. The first two or three just through the skin behind the thickest part. The last one, the 'top' maggot is hooked in the same way but the hook is pushed through a little further: *the point and the barb may show*. I do not believe this to be a disadvantage. Maggots often have a fairly thick skin, and if the point of the hook is hidden, the point may not penetrate easily. In any case all fish are accustomed to taking prickly food from time to time.

Photo 4. Bread-ball, containing a number of maggots. Placed on the lake bottom, the bread will slowly disintegrate: the maggots will crawl out and lure the bream or other fish to your baited hook. In calm weather it is also advisable to scatter a few maggots round your float. Don't forget that casters also make excellent bait.

N.B. Lack of space prevents my going into detail on the subject of bait, but the following general tips may be useful. When ground-baiting, always try to include a quantity of your hook bait. Ground-bait intelligently: having selected a good spot, first ground-bait all over, then drop an occasional rapidly disintegrating small bait ball. In some waters, where large shoals of bream strip the bottom, extra ground-baiting is desirable.

Photographs 5, 6 and 7 are of situations familiar to every bream fisher and require little comment, although they may provide some useful information on landing a fish.
Photo 5. Like most other fish, a bream should not be brought in until it is lying on its side.
Photo 6. The fish is drawn head forward towards the landing net, of which only the far edge is submerged in the water. When the entire fish lies above the net, this far edge is lifted and the net is drawn ashore through the water.

Photo 7. Bream leave an unpleasant layer of slime in the net. This should be rinsed off immediately, and at home the landing net should be thoroughly cleaned in hot salt water.
Unless this is done you will always have a smelly net.
Photo 8. A fine photograph of *Abramis brama* being unhooked. The closeup shows a remarkable phenomenon. In 1972 spring came very late and this bream has not yet lost the bumps which cover the heads and backs of male fish in the mating season.
Nowhere are bream very popular for eating, although, the author considers fishcakes

5

6

made from bream can be delicious if properly prepared.

In angling, experiment is the spice of life. A well-known fellow angler has introduced me to a system of bream fishing which has opened up entirely new perspectives. Bream will visit baited ground, but very large bream are particularly shy and will keep well away from an angler's boat. In order to catch these fish at some 15–20 yards from a boat (or from the shore, provided the angler has the wind in his back), the baited hook is cast over a thoroughly ground-baited area at this distance, with the bait at about 2 inches from the bottom shot. When the float cocks, the angler waits patiently, while very quietly taking in the slack on his line. The strike should be delayed until the float disappears: in this case this is done by firmly swinging the rod upwards and back. One of my friends has designed the perfect rod for this purpose, a soft actioned rod, which enables the angler to cast a bait, including flake or soft paste, to this distance without it dropping from the hook. He also uses a special float which is attached to the line by the bottom ring and can be used as a sliding float in deep water, or as a fixed float in shallow water.

Photo 9. A big bream from a reservoir.
Photo 10. The special float is here used as a sliding float: it is attached to the line only by the bottom ring.

9

10

11

12

Photo 11. The float is shotted and adjusted in such a way that it will just sink. The angler overcasts into deeper water so that it sinks, then draws it towards him until the tip is just visible above the water.

Photo 12. A bream has taken the bait. The shotting, within a couple of inches of the hook, is lifted, and the float rises and then keels over but the angler must be patient. It is essential to wait until the float disappears or – as occasionally happens – travels on the surface towards the angler. Meanwhile the angler has reeled in the slack of the line and at the right moment he strikes by firmly pulling back the tip of the rod. Tests have shown that in this method a long fully actioned rod is infinitely more effective at striking than a short one, especially when, as mentioned above, the fish swims towards the angler.

A word about experimenting

This might be an appropriate moment to say something about experimenting. It is a well-known fact that anglers in general – and bream fishers in particular – are rather conservative creatures. Nevertheless, the thought is gaining ground that we are too much inclined to stick to the same basics. What, after all, is the purpose of our sport? Simply to catch more fish? I do not think so. I believe that two points should be borne in mind. Firstly, we do our best to catch larger specimens. Secondly – a factor not to be ignored – many anglers, including myself, carry out experiments for their own sake. For instance, several days before I go out fishing I start to consider how I can change my methods. Sometimes it actually keeps me awake at night. In fact this advance preoccupation is a pleasure in itself. Strange to say it often comes to nothing, since, in spite of my love of experiment, I am at heart a lazy angler. Despite this I warmly recommend it. There are branches of the sport – deep-sea fishing, for instance – in which it must be possible by more active methods to achieve better results than is the case with current techniques.

To come back to freshwater angling.

In the final photographs in this chapter we return to the bream (and the bream fisher).

Photo 13. A familiar picture of a peaceful scene on and near the water. The angler's umbrella, and other types of shelter more recently are becoming popular. The writer has for years used a 'brolly' with great satisfaction. It keeps off the wind as well as the rain. The umbrella in the picture has the added advantage that it can be fixed sideways.

Photo 14. The bream has given up the struggle and is ready to be drawn out of the water.

Photo 15 shows a close-up of a fair-sized fish. Many anglers, however, have difficulty in distinguishing the small common bream from the silver bream. The following are some of the distinguishing marks:
Common bream: 27–28 rays in the anal fin: 49–57 scales along the lateral line: one row of teeth in the throat.
Silver bream: 22–26 rays in the anal fin: 55 scales along the lateral line: two rows of teeth in the throat.
In addition the silver bream has much larger eyes than the common bream.

15

Photo 16, finally, is a trick snapshot, taken with a so-called 'fish-eye' lens.

16

Carp

Wild carp though small are better fighters than the hatchery-bred fish used for stocking. Nonetheless, the latter provide good sport. In any case, how many anglers have the opportunity to lay siege to – let alone catch – the former? Photographs 1, 2 and 3 show fine mirror carp.

The mirror carp has one or two rows of scales along the lateral line: the leather carp is scaleless. The general characteristic of the common carp (*Cyprinus carpio*), the two long and the two short barbels on the upper lip, distinguish it from another fish with which it can be confused when small. This is the crucian carp. (*Carassius carassius*), occasionally caught in muddy water lacking in oxygen. The latter has no barbels.

Striking, playing and landing carp

Frequently the angler is a little too impatient in striking when he has a bite. The correct moment depends entirely on the size of bait and the manner of the bite, which might be very tentative indeed where the fish are heavily fished for or frequently caught. If the fish in question are not known to have been 'fished to death', striking may be delayed a little longer. As regards bait: if worms or maggots are used it is not necessary to strike quite as quickly as in the case of potato, which in turn does not necessitate the same immediate strike as bread or – even more so – paste.

In general it may be said that in the case of a fish like carp, which shows itself often, it is better not to strike immediately, but rather to wait patiently until the float disappears permanently under water (usually

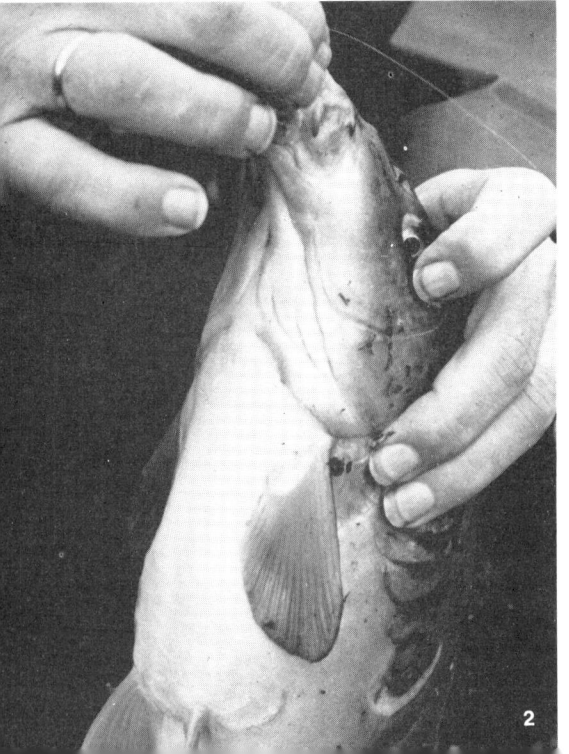

slowly and obliquely), or when fishing without a float, line runs off the spool. So much for theory. I have seen an – un-expected – strike from the common carp which was a veritable explosion. It happened in a mill-stream: I was fishing with two rods and before I could get hold of the carp rod, the fish had moved away with the speed of an express train and it was too late. The bait was a piece of potato. Since then I have never used a carp rod as a second rod with a closed bale-arm. Carp fishing requires complete concentration if it is to be done properly. Once the strike has been successfully carried out at the correct moment, the battle – in nine cases out of ten – starts in earnest. Hatchery-bred carp, too, which are used to stock some waters, know how to fight, especially the fully scaled carp. Let's have a look at the photographs.

Photograph 4: Playing a big fish with a fixed spool reel requires the use of a method known as 'pumping'. Keeping the line taut, the angler winds as he lowers the rod angle towards the water, but not to the extent of pointing the rod down the line. Then, with index finger pressed against the spool edge to stop it slipping, the angler pulls the rod towards the vertical, thus drawing in the fish a couple of feet. Should the fish make a run, the index finger pressure is eased and the fish takes off. Keep the clutch set reasonably lightly and *don't* try to wind against a tight line or a running fish or you will kink the line. Only wind while lowering the rod.

Never try to net a fish until it is completely played out and lying on its side. Do not be too gentle during the fight. Make it work

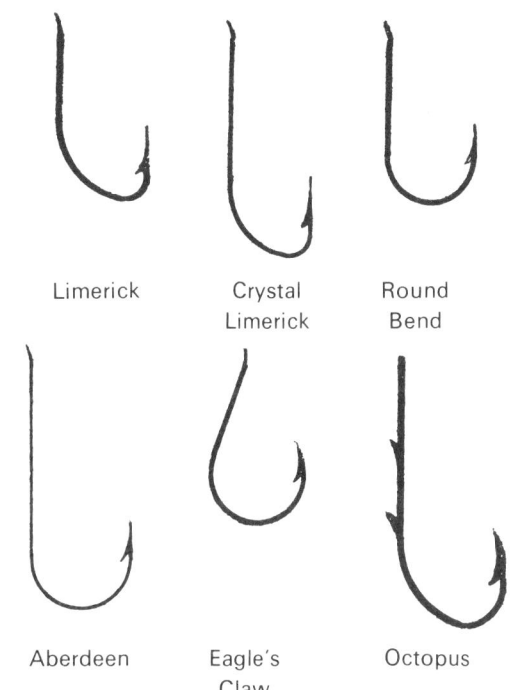

Limerick   Crystal Limerick   Round Bend

Aberdeen   Eagle's Claw   Octopus

4

5

hard to retain its position in its element and make it work hard for every inch of line it takes. And, of course, when fishing for big carp, make sure you have a net that's a big one. With an extra large fish you cannot have a net too large, but you can always have one that's too small.

The greatest danger occurs when a still powerful fish swims towards you (photo 5). Chase it away, for you will then be in a better position to impose your will on it. However, where carp is concerned there is one exception to the rule that the line should be kept taut. If you are unable to prevent the fish approaching an obstacle, for instance lily pads or posts, you should immediately pay out more line. If

a fish feels no resistance, it may well turn in its tracks (photo 6).

To summarise: draw the fish towards the net when the time is ripe and never try to scoop it up. Do not lift the fish above water (this applies to any heavy fish), but draw the net towards you and then land it with a steady lift (photo 7, p. 59).

Photograph 8 shows a carp perfectly hooked: a single hook just behind the hard lip. In this case the hook is easily removed and here it is done at the correct moment, namely, while the fish is still in the net. If the hook has caught deeper, do not start pulling, but use a disgorger. I personally favour the surgical forceps illustrated in use in photograph 13 (p. 27).

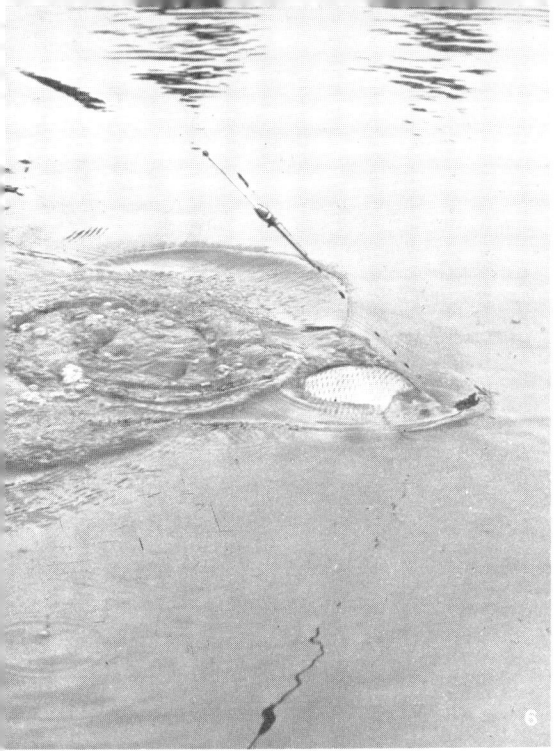

Photograph 9 shows a lady angler playing a fish at night, when many carp are caught, the hours of darkness often affording better fishing than during daylight.

It is understandable that the angler likes to be photographed with his catch (although I'm not fond of those unnecessary newspaper photographs of proud fishermen and the enormous fish they have caught). The angler in photograph 10 shows the fish in the correct manner, and what is more, he is releasing one correctly (photo 11), that is, not with an almighty splash, but very gently. Not only will this cause the least possible damage to the fish: it also avoids all unnecessary noise and disturbance. Always pick up the fish with wet hands and hold it firmly but not tightly. If you drop it, it is bound to be damaged.

Just like most other fish, carp may cause the angler many a surprise. One of my friends has on many occasions caught a carp while fishing for pike with artificial bait. 'Nothing unusual in that', you will say. "Obviously the bait caught in the carp's back or tail." This did in fact occasionally happen, but on other occasions carp — one a specimen of over 20 lb — were properly hooked with the bait (Mepps No. 3) in the upper lip. I might not have believed it if I had not seen it with my own eyes. How can this be explained?

Actually it is not all that difficult. Officially carp is not classified as a predatory fish,

but in fact all fish are predatory. What is more, every fish is a cannibal of the worst possible kind. In the case of carp there is further proof of this fact. If you use a floating bread-crust as bait — a method far too rarely used — you will find it is first taken by small roach. Suddenly they stop biting: this is the moment to be on your guard. It is possible that a pike or a bream is foraging, but it is even more probable that a large carp is approaching. That the same applies to other fish as well is proved by the fact that I myself have repeatedly caught rudd with spinning baits and I have seen one of my friends catch a magnificent specimen with the well-known 'Flopy'. This was no coincidence, for having missed the first time, the fish immediately took on the second cast.

Just a word about keeping away troublesome duck and swans. Never offer them bread or any other food — they will persist in plaguing you. A fellow-angler has invented a good method. Although he always fishes for carp with floating bread-crusts, the ducks avoid him: they have learnt from experience that he always has a catapult and a supply of earth handy...

Tench

The tench (*Tinca tinca*) is a curious and somewhat mysterious fish, which has been called by many names and about which the most remarkable tales have been (and are) told. For instance, it was supposed to act as 'doctor' to other fish, as its slimy skin is said to have healing powers.

The tench is eagerly pursued in this country and there is an organisation called 'The Tenchfishers' who specialise in catching very big tench and learning all they can about their quarry and the techniques to catch them. They *do* catch large tench too! The author often fishes for tench because the fish intrigues him. Light tackle in open water will give grand sport, for tench will be found in open shallow, muddy, weed-free areas, and deep water too, although it is often associated with patches of weeds and waterplants in lakes and ponds where heavier tackle is necessary. It is also found in slow-moving waters.

Bait: preferably a good-sized worm: if there are too many small perch about, a good-sized bread flake or a big bundle of maggots will do the trick. One might also clear a few square yards of weed from a shallow pond: when the area is ground-baited, tench will usually put in an appearance pretty soon. Where shot is not absolutely necessary to sink the bait quickly, it should be placed as high on the line as possible. A hook with a leaded shank is useful for catching under duckweed. Bait the hook with a large worm and move it across the surface of the duckweed, trying to make the worm hop like a frog. Then allow the bait to sink through the duck-weed where it will soon be firmly taken — sometimes this happens immediately. Perch and pike frequently fall for this tempting ruse.

When you use ordinary tackle and a float, tench will sometimes react in an entirely different manner. In that case they may behave with great caution, first dithering the float a few times before taking the bait. It is therefore not easy to distinguish between the bite of a tench and that of an eel. In any case the strike should be delayed until the float disappears. It is easy enough to await the correct moment when using worm or maggots, but angling with bread requires a certain amount of experience.

I should just mention that I have on occasion taken a tench with a piece of potato when fishing for carp.

The four photographs speak for themselves. A tench is recognised by its strong, broad and unforked tail.

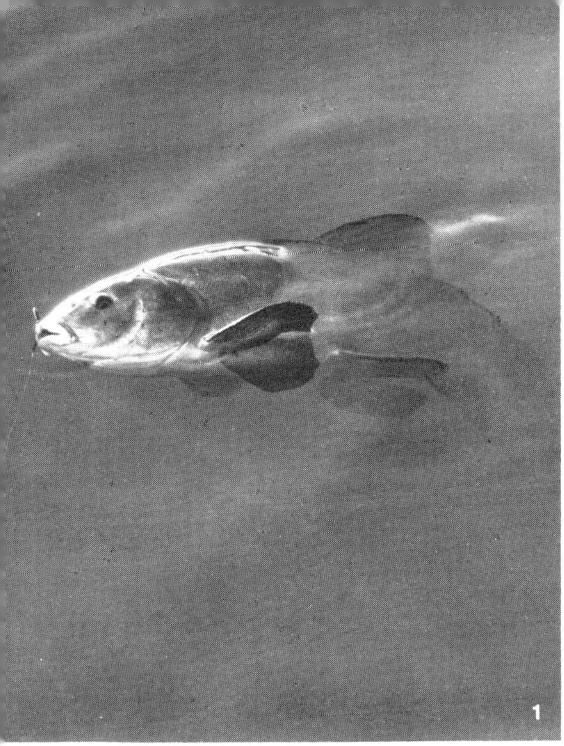
1

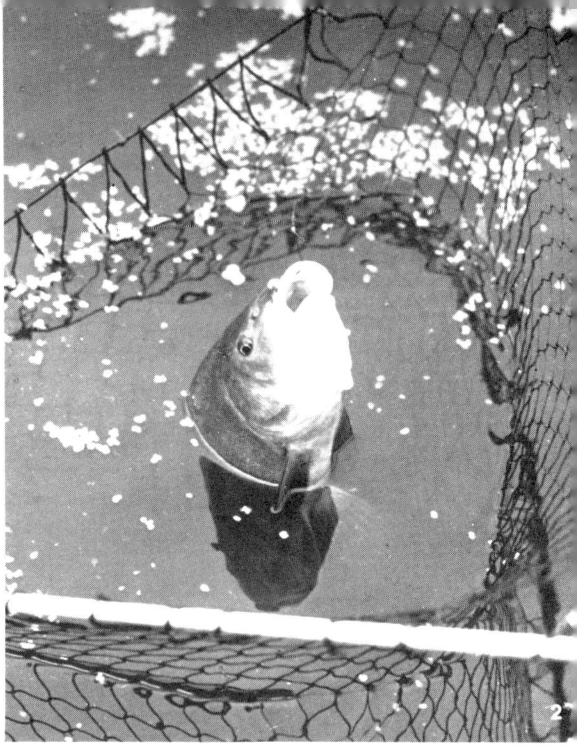
2

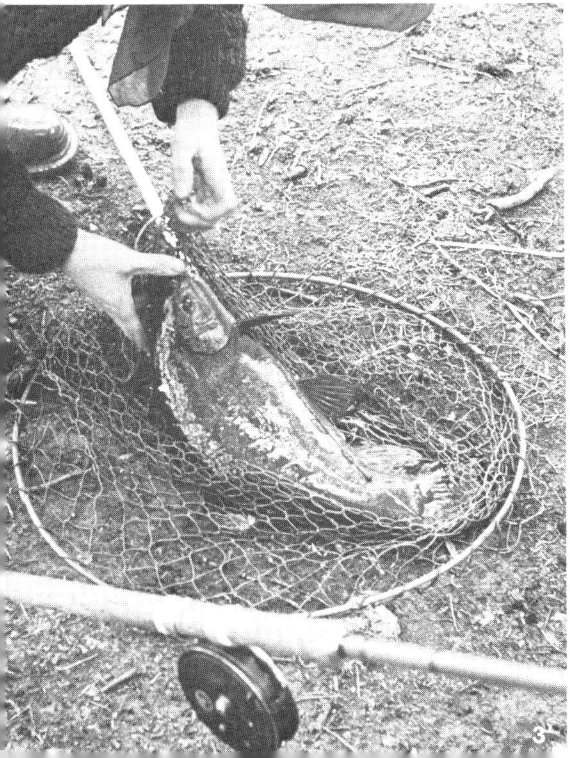
3

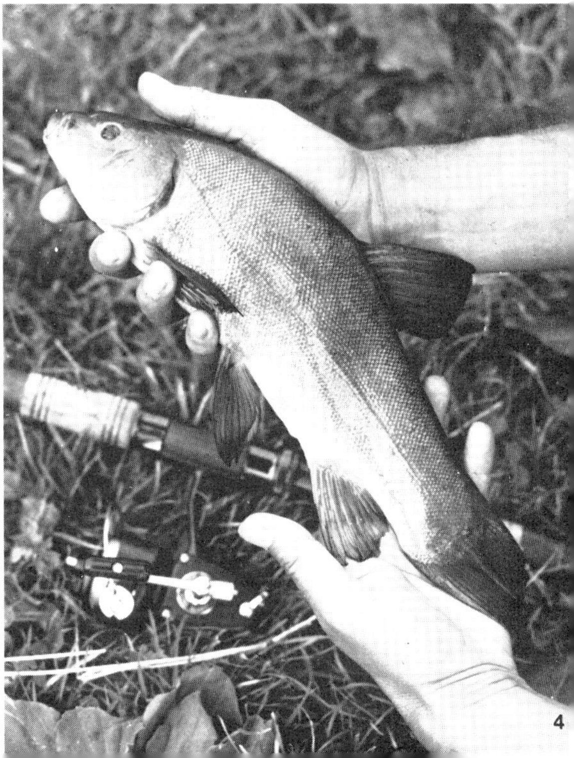
4

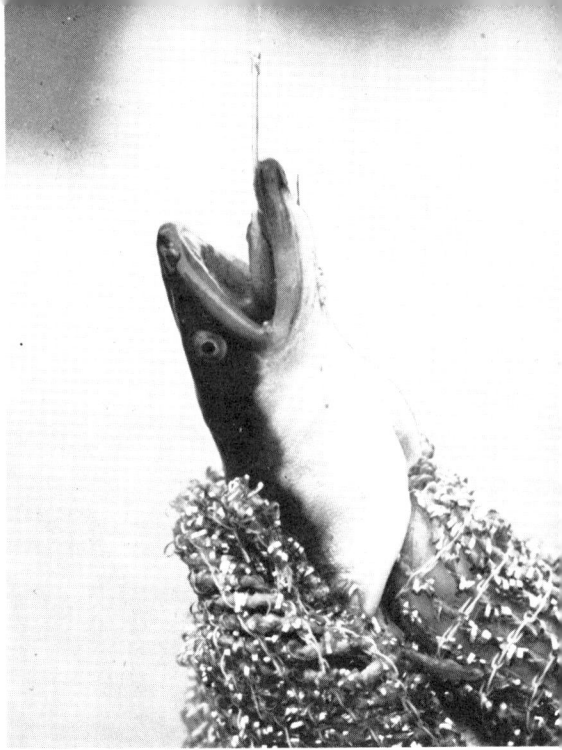

1

Eel

This fish (*Anguilla anguilla*) presents us with quite a few problems. (Quite apart from its price on the market – it is a mystery why this fish, which is, after all, quite plentiful, if anglers wished to catch them, should be so expensive). Most anglers have no doubt on occasion been guilty of unparliamentary language when the thinnest of eels has so tangled up his line that cutting it was the only solution. It is, moreover, by no means easy to pinpoint the habitat of this fish, although one general guideline exists. Since the eel is a great roe-eater, it will be obvious that, especially in spring, it will be found in those places where other fish deposit their spawn, that is, near the stalks of water-plants, especially in shallows along the banks. There are various ways in which it may be caught. The most usual method is with a bottom rod and not too thin a line – the eel is capable of hanging on to any available support in the most remarkable manner. Hook: an ordinary coated eel hook, or a medium-sized Aberdeen. Bait: worm, a very small dead fish, and in some places salt herring. Apparently the fellow likes matured cheese, slightly soaked, as well, but I have no personal experience of this bait.

When fishing for eels in deep water, or, for instance, in an estuary, many people use

a light beach rod, leger lead, and a bite indicator.

Photo 1. A typical example. A fat eel, firmly held in a glove-shaped pot-scourer, managed to get its tail under the angler's watch-strap and nearly broke it. Hard to believe – but true!

Photo 2. The eel was finally overcome. Eel is killed by a few blows with a heavy object about the area of the vent.

Photo 3. Tongs, easily made, can be very useful for picking up and holding an eel, although experienced eelcatchers are able to subdue even the fattest eel with one

hand. It looks a lot easier than it is.

Photo 4. This eel was caught on a mackerel fishing trip, but make no mistake: the eel we take from the estuaries is not the true sea-eel (*Conger conger*), which usually occurs in deep waters.

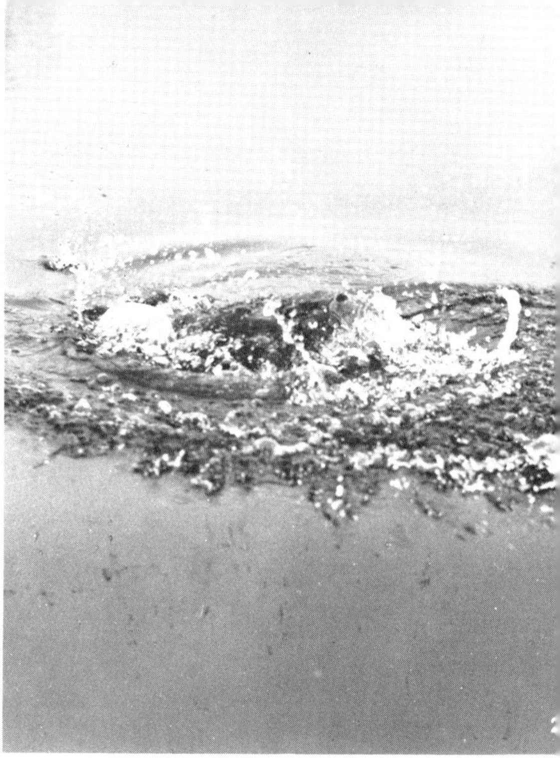

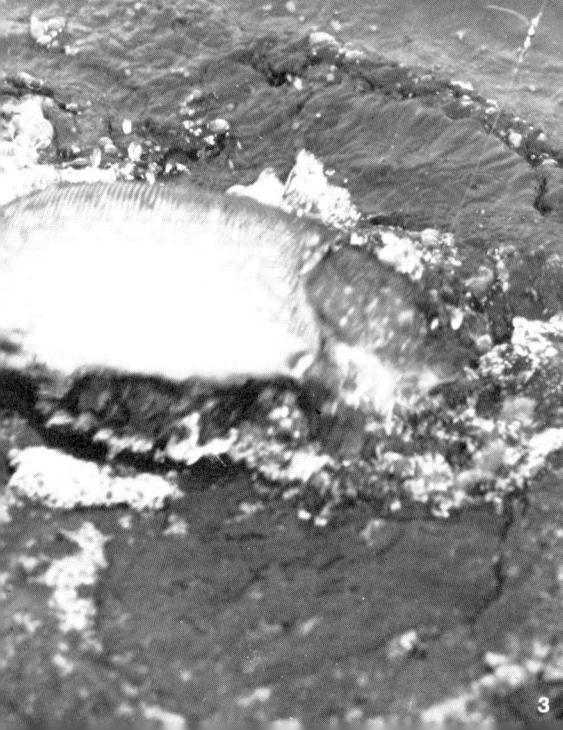

Pike

To fish for pike (*Esox lucius*), you'll first have to find it. As I said in the introduction to this book, it is important to know something about a fish's way of life and its feeding habits: this will make it easier to get on its tracks. Pike may be roughly divided into two categories: the hunters and the lurkers. The former are slightly smaller and roam the waters to find their food: the latter are the big ones (often females) who have found a good feeding spot, well hidden and at the same time serving as a refuge. All pike are somewhat lazy by nature. They do not pursue their prey for long, but rather lie in wait, like a cat. Pike should therefore be sought behind a tree that has fallen in the water, behind a sunken boat, in the narrows of a stream or under a hollow bank, to mention but a few places. In waters with a fairly smooth bank, such as that in photograph 1, it is necessary to investigate the various possibilities slowly and quietly. Patience is of the essence, whether you are angling with fish bait or with a lure. This applies even when two or three pike fishers follow each other at short intervals. The third will have the same, or even better, chance than the first. There is some truth in the saying: "The first man dislodges the pike, the second arouses its curiosity and the third catches it."

Photograph 2 shows how strongly a pike can resist. (Even though it lacks the staying powers of the carp). An experienced angler will be able to tell from the bite whether he has caught a large or a small pike, especially when using live bait. If the float disappears slowly and at an angle, it's most likely a big one, but if the pike float jumps about impetuously the size of the pike will usually be disappointing. The vehement snatch is probably intended to paralyse the prey by fright.

The pike in photograph 7 was caught using a small fish hooked in the back. Many anglers make a slight mistake here, which may lead to disappointment. They believe that they should strike immediately the fish has bitten, since it takes the bait in the back and must therefore have the hook in its mouth. However, as a rule, *Esox* takes its prey in the same way as does a hound: it bites strongly, lets go for an instant and only then takes the bait properly. You should therefore wait a moment before striking, even although the bait fish has been hooked in the back.

Some anglers may not have a wish to use a *live* fish as bait for pike for ethical reasons, and yet fail to be very successful with artificial baits such as spoons, plugs, etc. There is an alternative which has become increasingly popular in England, which is fishing with dead fish. One doesn't even need to catch fish to use as bait. Spratts and sardines can be purchased from the fish shop; and if larger baits are required, herrings and mackerel are popular. All of these, unnatural baits for freshwater, and others, have tempted a great many very large pike, and many more of lesser proportions.

The manner in which most anglers fish with a dead bait is to simply cast out to an area where it is considered pike will be, allowing the dead bait to sink to the bottom and lie there until it is picked up by a roving pike. A lazy way to fish for a big lazy fish

that's too lazy to hunt for live food! Certainly, static dead bait fishing does seem to sort out the big ones.

The bale-arm of a fixed-spool reel is left in the open position, or multiplier or centre-pin reel is adjusted to freely revolve, so that when a pike picks up a bait and moves off, it can do so freely until the angler sets the hook. Two small treble hooks in tandem make a suitable hook arrangement.

Photograph 3 shows that the pike does not yet intend to give up the struggle. It may leap several times, fleeing in all directions, as is done by a hare, and trying to dislodge the hook. The angler should always be prepared for these manœuvres.

In photograph 4, the struggle is almost at an end and the pike begins to lie on its side. Pike should always be de-hooked with care, for jaws, palate and the interior of the gill covers are all covered in vicious teeth, pointing towards the rear. The pike-gags on the market simplify the operation, but sometimes I prefer to use a matchbox, used lengthways or sideways, depending on the size of the fish (photo 5). If it is a large fish the use of a gag becomes essential, but remember, damage may be avoided by first filing down the sharp points of the instrument. Always hold a pike – even a dead one – by the back (photo 6), never with the fingers under the gill covers.

The pike in photograph 8 has been caught with a leaded spinner. Many anglers prefer

this type because it is easy to cast, but actually it is suitable also for deep or fast-running water.

But whatever spinner you use, you should reel in very slowly. Nearly all pike fishers ignore this rule, forgetting that the pike is a lazy fish. Vary the speed from time to time and occasionally draw the bait sideways, even when using a lure. Make sure the blade is turning freely, and afterwards clean the lure thoroughly. When pike-fishing in large, deep waters, I would recommend plug bait every time. Correctly presented, it is a lethal weapon. A plug does not spin, but wobbles. Make your cast, let the plug sink for a moment, draw back slightly obliquely, sink again, straight

down, etc. Often the fish will bite just when the plug swirls downwards. The large wobbling spoon is also excellent for pike.

Some technical details and gadgets for use in pike fishing

Photograph 9 shows various spoon baits. The upper one, with blade, turns slowly and runs deep, creating strong vibrations. The second has a narrow blade, turns rapidly and runs a little higher. The lower specimen is weighted (particularly suitable for deep or fast-running water). The small fly spinner has more than once yielded a fine pike, although intended for use with

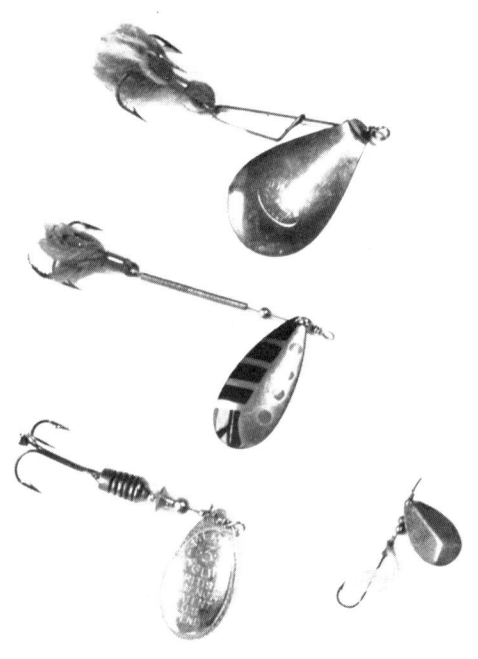

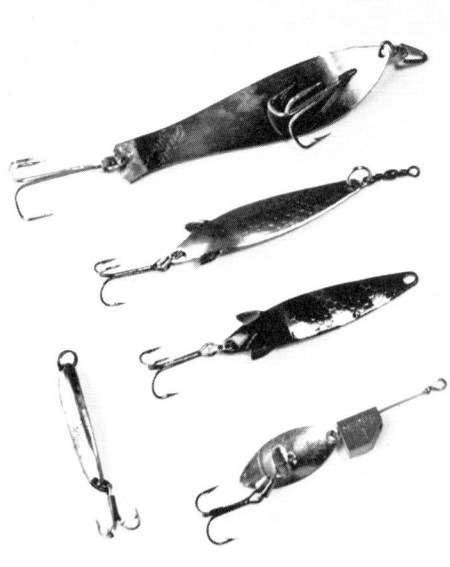

an ultra-light rod and the smallest of reels, in fishing for rudd, perch or trout. Small sizes of the three lower types are also very suitable for perch and trout fishing.

Photograph 10 shows a number of lures and requires no comment, while in photograph 11 you see some plugs which, because of their adjustable diving vanes, may be presented at a high level ready for diving or swimming deep. I have had good results with the lower lure, the 'Flopy', which is made of rubber: but not everyone shares my opinion and experience.

As a rule pike fishers use a wire trace to prevent the line being bitten through by the fish's sharp teeth. This kind of trace is marketed in many forms, but I particularly like the Berkley 'Steelon leader' which enables the angler to construct his own traces to any desired length. (Ready-made leaders are to my mind often too short.) This trace wire is supplied in reels of 25 feet and the crimps can be purchased separately. Photograph 12 shows the closing of a crimp. Berkley traces may also be bought readymade in two lengths.

Photograph 13. The 'Jardine' snap-tackle is a simple, widely used tackle, that has stood the test of more than three-quarters of a century.

Photograph 14 shows, anti-kink spinning leads: to be attached above the wire trace. The fold-over half-moon leads are simply pressed on the line. With moving leger

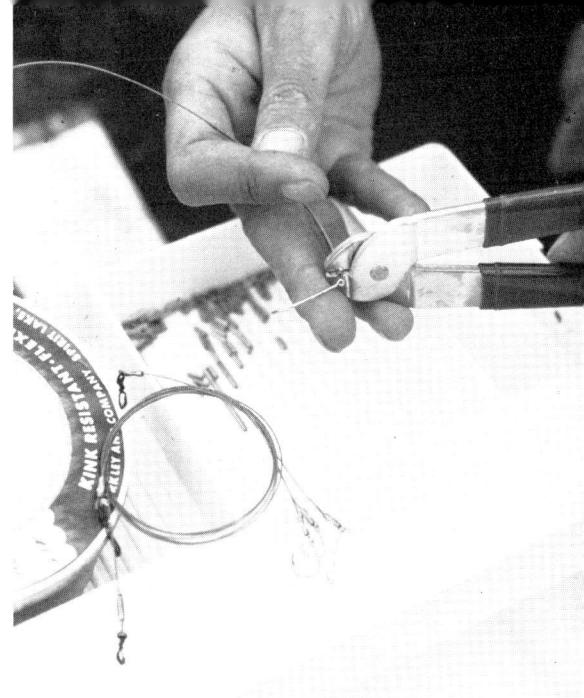

technique, in which the bottom of a pool or lake is slowly explored, a fish bait is always hooked through the nostril (photo 15, p. 73). When the pike bites, the line runs through a pear lead without resistance.

Photo 16 (p. 73) shows various pike floats. The one farthest right is a *Fishing Gazette* type, the centre one and those above are sliders through which the line can slide for fishing deep water. I believe the middle left one to be the best. This is a plastic 'tubed' float – which by inserting the stem or not, may be used either as a fixed or as a sliding float. It is visible from a considerable distance if fished high, and I find it most satisfactory.

There is a certain amount of misunderstanding concerning both pike and pike fishing. To begin with, *Esox* is regarded as the biggest predator in our waters, but in fact it is not. In my opinion the eel is worse. This latter fish is moreover very fond of spawn and can therefore be disastrous to fish stocks. The story that a pike eats its own weight in food every day is another myth. It eats proportionately less than a human being. Another error concerns the size of prey a pike is able to deal with. I know the fish lack fear and, like me, you may have seen photographs of a pike choked in its efforts to swallow an only slightly smaller fellow-pike. I once caught a pike only just above the legal limit which had an almost fully grown rat in its stomach. There are stories about pike biting cows in the nose, pulling sheep into the water or attacking swimmers – but do you believe these? I do know one good anecdote. In Holland, the owner-manager of a swimming pool where fishing is also allowed, prohibits fish being taken away, but an exception is made for pike-perch, for on several occasions swimmers have had their toes bitten by these fish. This is a true story, not an angler's tale.

To come back to the pike. Nature itself has given it the marks of a predator and a hunter. This refers not only to its shape, which indicates speed, and its mouth lined with razor-sharp teeth angled backwards, but also to its mating and spawning seasons, which take place some time before the spawning time of other fish, with the result that young pike can eat the small fry of their fellow fish as soon as they leave the eggs.

This brings me back to the pike which had been choked by the body of another. I think that this was a case of rivalry rather than of gluttony. Especially in the mating season, *Esox* is inclined to attack anything suspicious that approaches.

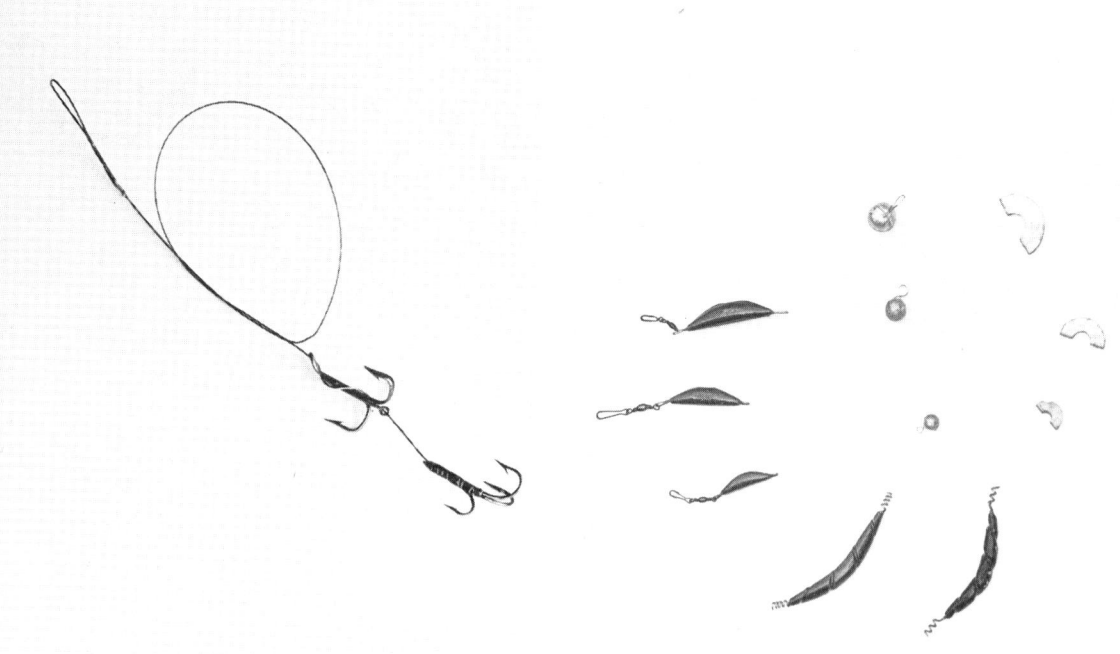

15

16

Perch

Perch (*Perca fluviatilis*) used to be a very popular fish in the angling world, but in recent years there has been some cause for concern, since their numbers are believed to have decreased. I am unable to confirm this, but it may reassure you to know that there are now encouraging reports from the lakes and reservoirs.

Appearance

If it were economically possible to print the photographs in this book in colour, the perch would undoubtedly qualify as a prize winner in a beauty competition. It is particularly beautiful when it rushes at its prey,

fins erect, or when it thrashes about in the landing net, furious at being caught. There is considerable variety in colour but a perch is easily recognised. It has a prickly dorsal fin with, as a rule, 15 spines (sometimes less) and five to nine transverse bands across the body. Photograph 4 gives a good idea of its appearance. The only correct way of holding it without hurting yourself is shown in photograph 6.

Photograph 7 is a very large perch weighing over 3 lb

There is a little fish which looks something like a perch called 'ruffe' or 'pope' (*Acerina cernua*), which is very prolific in some waters, taking worm or maggot avidly. If you are catching these you will be well

74

advised to go elsewhere as you will not catch many other fish where ruffe abound.

Habitat and mode of life

Unlike the pike which, as said earlier, is a fairly lazy fish, perch hunt for their food, although the manner in which they do so varies. Small to medium-sized perch, like mackerel, hunt in shoals, driving small fish before them. I have often seen this happening in reservoirs, when the startled small fry were jumping out of the water in their dozens. A knowledgeable angler will deduce the presence of perch from the behaviour of small fish being herded into corners of a lake or actually jumping out on to the bank. A similar phenomenon may be observed when pike-perch are feeding, but in that case only a few small fry are being hunted instead of entire shoals. In streams, canals, etc., perch are usually found near posts and shored up banks, especially near camp sheathing used under water to protect banks. In an old but useful book I read that perch are attracted by bundles of twigs in the water, and especially by recently tarred lock-gates, etc. Try placing a newly tarred stick in the water to attract the fish. Some anglers in fact include tar in their bait mixture. Perch is easily found in slow flowing waters, where it lives close to weedbeds and lily pads, although it likes to have a stretch of open water nearby.

It should be noted that very large perch prefer solitude and, except in the mating season, hunt alone, although I believe that they are never far away from shoals, in order to profit from the hunted small fry. N.B. I say this from experience, for it can hardly be a coincidence that often, when fishing for 'shoal-fish' I caught extra large specimens by taking a chance and casting a few yards away from a baited swim. It is worth a try!

Fishing methods

There are several ways of catching perch with a bottom rod. Since large perch should be sought close to the bottom, I prefer to use a line with a few bubble floats, shotted in such a way that the lower two remain under water. Shot should be placed fairly close to the hook. Photograph 12 (p. 79) will give you an idea. With this tackle, and a big hook baited with one or two good-sized worms we explore the open spaces among the water plants. This method works well, since slight undulations of the bottom will not entail repeated adjustment of a float.

Talking of worms, a word about the way they should be hooked. In photographs 9, 10 and 11 you will see how I do it. The hook is inserted behind the head of the worm, which is then pushed on the shank. Often one worm seems too small and in that case I do it as follows. The point of

5

6

the hook emerges halfway down the first worm: the next one is hooked in exactly the same way, and finally the point of the hook is inserted in the tail of number one. Photograph 11 shows the wriggling worm bundle thus created. Of course there are other ways of doing it, but the above method has always been found to be very satisfactory.

Naturally the predatory perch may equally well be caught with a small live fish bait: the method is the same as in pike fishing, although it is not necessary to use a wire trace. In my experience perch bites more decisively than pike. On the other hand it often takes a fish larger than it can cope with: when that happens, the bait is quickly abandoned. However, in waters where large perch may be expected, I like to use a fairly sizeable bait-fish – about 4 inches, for instance. It is difficult to be specific as regards the breaking strain of the line.

Perch is a particularly attractive opponent when angling with spinners, for it will take nearly any kind. Many anglers like to use a spinner with the hook partially concealed in a pluck of wool, preferably red in colour. I have never found this particularly attractive to perch, and personally achieve good results with weighted spinners such as the Mepps (in deep water) and with the attractive spoons with a fly tied to the hooks as shown in photograph 8. Any ethical fisherman will of course replace the treble hook with a single. Naturally there are many other, equally good, types of artificial bait. Unlike the pike, perch sometimes has a habit of swimming after the artificial bait and even pushing it with its nose, without biting. In that case it may help to pull it away quickly. I would in any case advise repeated variations in speed when angling for perch with artificial bait. If *Perca* still does not bite, the hook might be baited with a worm.

In large waters, where the bottom is not too foul, the use of a paternoster may be rewarding when fishing for perch. This is often done with a spinning rod. A pear-shaped lead is hung on the end of the line:

two or three short links with baited hooks (usually worms) are attached above. Cast, then gently reel in. Perch will bite fiercely.

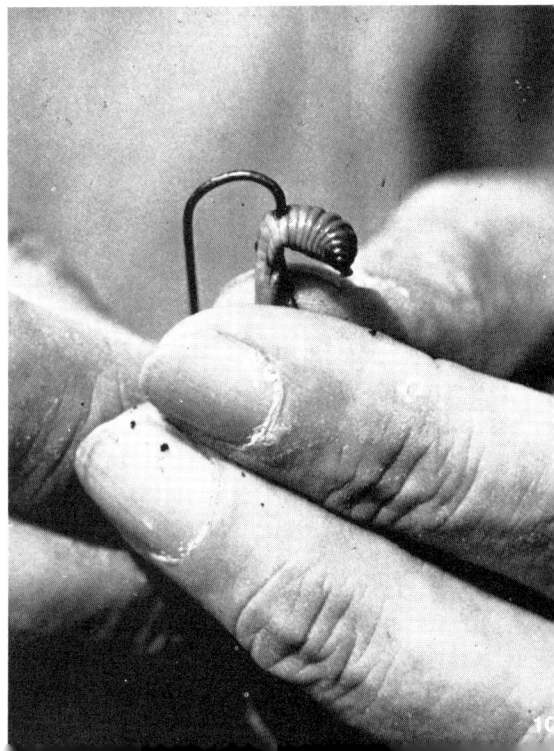

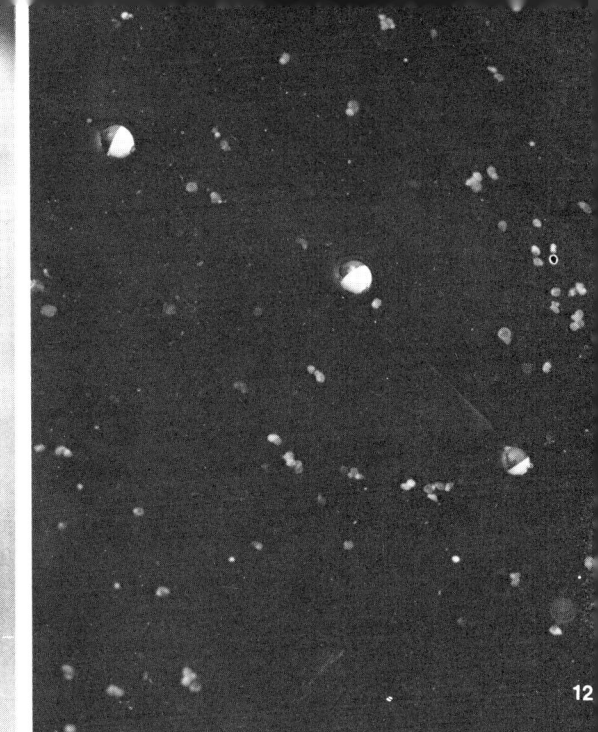

Pike-perch

Every angler knows that pike-perch or zander (*Lucioperca lucioperca*) is not a cross between pike and perch, but in this country there are plenty of anglers who have never seen, let alone caught, this capricious fish. To them I would say: if you go to the right area — the Fens, and hook a fish which is shaped like a pike but has a perch's prickly dorsal fin, you will have caught *Lucioperca*. This fine fish, very good to eat, is becoming more and more 'fashionable' as the pike population in these overfished waters declines, although the idea that pike and pike-perch do not tolerate each other's presence may be considered a myth. I have often caught both in the same place, using the same bait. Pike-perch is portrayed in the photograph on p. 8.

As I said, pike-perch is a capricious fish, not only in its biting habits, but also as regards its habitat. Probably the only thing that may be said with certainty is that it is found close to the bottom, usually in deep water, but occasionally in shallow spots as well. As usual, exceptions confirm the rule...

It is therefore not surprising that there are various ways of catching this fish, and adherents of the various methods are wrong in advocating theirs as the only possible one. I should just like to mention the method used by a well-known fellow-angler, who has a deserved reputation in this respect.

Photo 3. Pike-perch is not consistent in the way in which it takes live bait, but in my experience it usually does so from the rear.

I therefore always start by hooking the bait fish in the tail. If this is unsuccessful I vary the method.

Photo 4. In many waters the 'jig' (the two lower leaded streamers) and any standard 'streamer' are excellent lures for pike-perch. Large perch also go for these.

Let me start by telling you that this man who trolls from a boat in lakes, always begins his fishing exploits by thoroughly sounding the depth of the water until he knows the 'underwater landscape' like the back of his hand. As a rule he seeks and finds pike-perch near undulations of the bottom. He then fishes the suitable water inch by inch. I have often fished with him and know he misses nothing.

To digress for a moment. For this method of angling an electric engine such as the 'Wondertroll' by Noris Shakespeare is ideal (photos 5 and 6). It is completely noiseless and one may move as slowly as one likes. It has the possible disadvantage that it requires a battery which lasts for a maximum of about six hours, but a lot of water may be covered in that time.

To return to the expert's method.

It is very important to fish right on the bottom and to follow the contours of the lake bed very carefully. This latter is difficult without an echo sounder so it is wise to go over the ground *several* times where one has discovered the undulations. As one cannot see the bottom, nor mark the water surface with chalk, it is unlikely that one will follow the exact route as before, and so slightly different ground along the premised contour will be followed, but after a few 'runs' along the route, the water should have been fished pretty thoroughly.

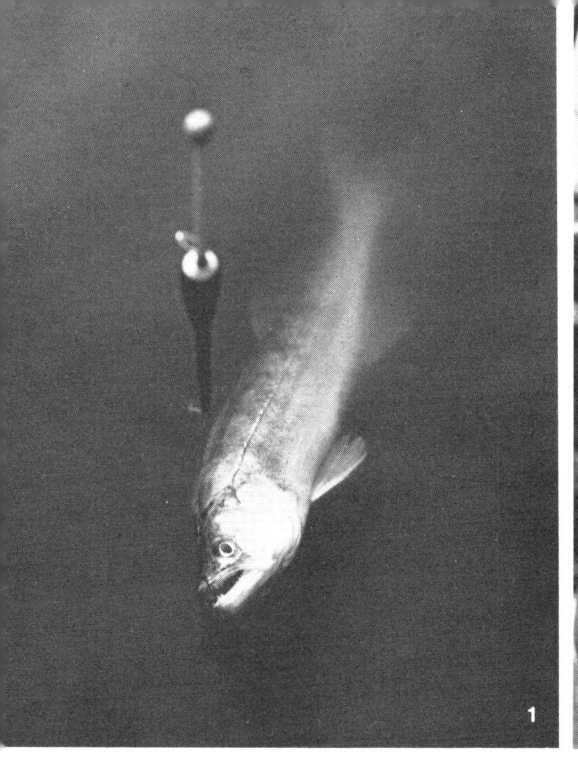

5

6

Troll very, very, slowly, and use a fairly heavy lead placed on the line a couple of yards above the bait. This is bounced along the bottom with the live or dead fish trailing behind.

The expert is, moreover, convinced that the bait (including dead fish) must always be kept moving to yield results.

Photo 7. A good rod support is essential in a boat. The Shakespeare Company manufacture an excellent model.

Photo 8. Sliding floats. Fellow-anglers have sometimes taunted me for using the uppermost one, which they call my 'whistling buoy', because of its size. However, it was specially made for me by a famous zander fisher and I have often had the last laugh . . .

7

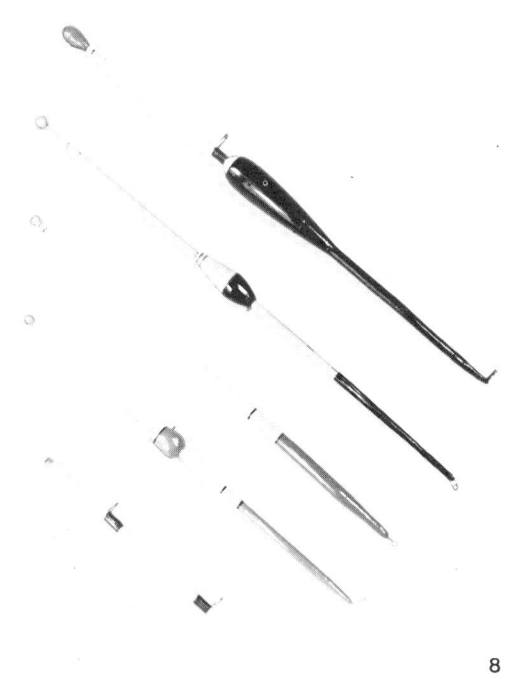

8

Trout

Trout fishing! An angler's face becomes transfigured on hearing these words. However, on the following pages I shall have some hard words to address to those anglers who declare carelessly: "Caught a few trout this week." To catch a trout in itself means nothing, for the trout in question are probably hatchery-bred specimens which are on the whole as easy, or even easier, to catch as many a native roach. I have seen trout being caught with the most unsuitable equipment.

Nevertheless I am not such a 'stick-in-the-mud' purist that I condemn anyone who tries to catch trout by other methods than with an artificial fly, or at any rate a spinner. As far as I'm concerned you may use a fish or a worm. No doubt this statement will earn me the wrath of many of my fellow anglers, but I don't very much mind. I have only one condition to make: give trout the chance to show its fighting qualities. Fish with subtlety and you will find the fish to be a worthy opponent.

Appearance

In this country we have two kinds of non-migratory trout. The rainbow trout (*Salmo gairdneri*) has a wide reddish (or even purplish) lateral band and black spots on the dorsal fin – normally on the tail as well. This trout is better able to endure slow-moving or stagnant water than the brown trout (*Salmo trutta*), which lacks the former's magnificent colouring, but equals its fighting powers. It should be mentioned in passing that, although the rainbow trout is good to eat, most people much prefer the brown trout.

Fishing methods

Trout is a tremendous hunter and predator, and is by no means choosy in its feeding habits. It may therefore be caught by the same methods as, say, the rudd, but take my advice and only fish for trout in such a way that you may be justifiably proud of it – preferably with a fly. For fly-fishing, see pp. 34–41.

In many stretches of shallow water, large areas may be covered by wearing wading boots (photo 6), or, even better, wading trousers if allowed, but good results may also be obtained by fly-fishing from the bank. Flies used for trout vary considerably in types and sizes, and can be fished on or just beneath the surface, or many feet deep.

Although trout fishing is becoming more and more popular, there are still many anglers who are unfamiliar with this branch of the sport. For beginners, where conditions permit, a light spinning rod with a line of 5 lb. breaking strain is very suitable. I have caught magnificent rainbow trout with a weighted spoon bait, which is easy to cast, namely Mepps no. 2. No. 3 has also yielded good results. Other types of the

same size will doubtless do equally well. Nevertheless I should like to advise you to try a small plug or a jig when fishing in deep water. Hatchery-bred trout released in such waters quickly lose the mode of life to which they were accustomed in their original environment, where they feed chiefly on the surface. They acquire the habits of bottom-feeders like the roach. Once, when fishing for eels in a deep channel in a large lake, I caught a rainbow trout which weighed over five pounds, and I freely confess that it ended up in the frying pan. It was pure luck! And finally a method I have never tried myself, since I prefer the fly and the spinner: the use of a worm, spinning or fishing sink-and-draw fashion, may give good results when fishing for trout from a suitable bank.

Photo 1. Fly fishing.
Photo 2. Spinning for trout.
Photo 3. The trout has been unable to resist the (fairly large) lure. Its fellow in photograph 4 is trying to regain its freedom by jumping.

5

6

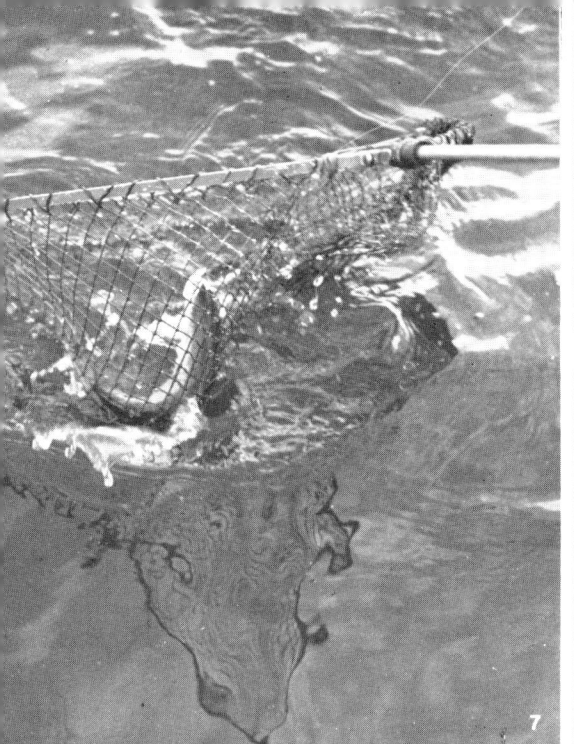

Photo 5. A trout to be proud of.
Photo 6. Wading helped catch this fine trout.
Photo 7. The trout is landed.
Photo 8. Fine brown trout.

PART 2

SEA

TECHNIQUE AND TACKLE

Double-handed sea-rod casting

Is it really necessary to learn this technique of casting? This is a question I am often asked and I'll do my best to answer it. The questioner's argument is quite simple: they have often caught more fish close to the shore than a supercaster who put his bait well over a hundred yards out.

The reason is obvious. There are times when fish like flounder and bass can be caught by the dozen in knee-deep water. But this is not what the sport is all about. Look at it like this: someone who is able to cast over a great distance can also bring his bait close to the shore, but the reverse is not the case.

I know dozens of places along the coast where long-distance casting will be successful in ninety out of a hundred cases, while it is useless to fish close to shore. This applies equally to inland waters.

It should be noted that, when fishing with lures, it is usually more important to place the cast correctly than to cover a great distance. I would therefore advise you to acquire the art of precision casting in single-handed casting. You will thus also avoid the risk of losing your spoon or spinner in the grass on the other bank of the stream when you are river fishing. Nevertheless, when fishing with a single-handed rod in the sea opportunities may occur where long-distance casting becomes essential; for instance, where the fish inhabit a deep gully which may be as much

as 100 yards or more from the shore. It is better then to change to a two-handed rod.

Photo 1. The angler faces the direction of the cast: the lead hangs directly below the tip of the rod.

Photo 2. The body is turned to the right at an angle of 90°. The angler lowers the lead to just under a yard from the ground, keeping everything in view.

Photos 3 and 4. As soon as the lead hangs still the cast is made – not a moment sooner or later.

Photo 5. The line is released at the exact moment when rod and line point out to sea.

Photo 6. When moving from position 3 to 4, the weight of the body is transferred from one leg to the other, while the feet remain in the same place. For left-handed anglers the positions are naturally reversed. The illustrations – particularly photographs 3 and 4 – show clearly that an adequately long reach is of great importance.

Long-distance casting is not as difficult as many anglers fear. Ask an expert friend to teach you, or better still, join an angling club if there is one in your neighbourhood.

The right choice of rod

This depends on the angler's individual circumstances. The rod shown in the six photographs on p. 91 is nearly 16 feet long: the angler's height is 6 feet. Shorter people will, of course, also be able to handle such a long rod, provided they are in good health and possess sufficient (i.e. normal) strength. The method illustrated is one of many, but it does lead to excellent results. The cast in the photographs,

carried out with a 8 oz. casting weight, reached 200 yards. This is more than the average fisherman will ever need: the most ambitious sea angler may be satisfied with a cast of 80–100 yards.

What struck me most when watching this cast was the quiet way in which it was carried out.

Fixed spool sea reels and multipliers

Sea reels are available in many price ranges. Whether you buy an expensive one or a cheaper version will depend in the first place on the contents of your pocket, and in the second place on how often you go sea fishing. Some boatmen who run angling charters have equipment for hire on board, but this often leaves a lot to be desired – hardly surprising when you consider that most people who hire this tackle are novices. A beginner would probably do best to buy a fixed spool reel with an automatic bale arm (photo 10).

Photo 7. A few excellent beachcasting rods by Modern Arms, and East Anglian Rod Co. There are many other equally good makes but it is impossible to mention them all.

Photo 8. Boatfishing rods. For big fish it is sometimes advisable to use a roller top ring, and if fishing with wire lines, roller rings all through are advisable, but at least the tip and butt rings.

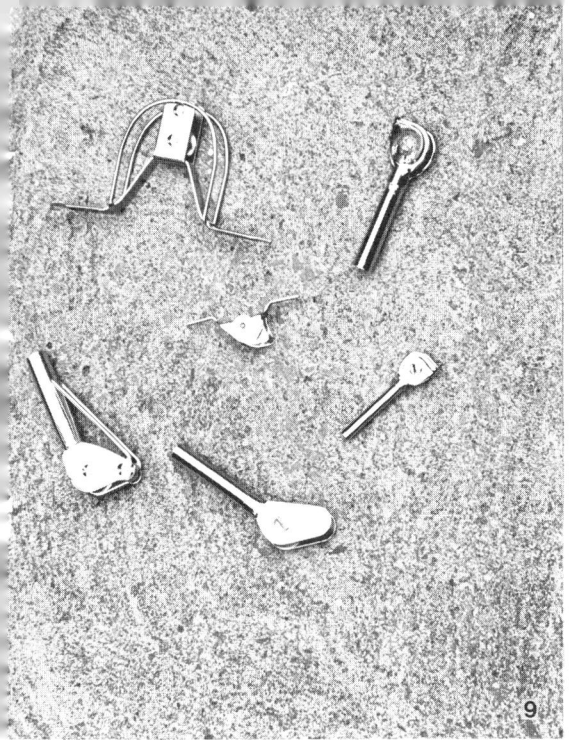

Photo 9. Good quality roller rings for boat rods. Expensive, but if looked after – well worth it!

Some experienced anglers prefer a finger pick-up rather than an automatic bale-arm when fishing with a fixed spool reel. Daiwa make such a model. There are also fixed spool reels available with skirted spools (photo 11), which arrest the possibility of line getting behind the spool and tangled around the reciprocating spindle.

Personally, I like to fish with a multiplying reel. Although the normal geared models cannot be wound in as fast as a fixed spool reel, it is possible to exert more power without damaging the mechanism. The multiplier in photograph 12 has a device that controls the spool speed during the cast, and stops it revolving upon the lead entering the water, thus eliminating over-runs. This device can be obtained from Don's Fishing Tackle, Fore Street, Edmonton, at a very reasonable price. Without such a device, the expert controls his cast by what is called an 'educated thumb', which is delicate thumb pressure upon the rotating spool during the cast, and instant hard pressure to stop the rotation when lead hits sea.

I should add that I have been using the 'Ambassador' multiplier (made by the Swedish firm A.B.U.) with great satisfaction. It is quite expensive, but is one of the best. The same applies to the 'Ambassador'

freshwater multiplier made by the same firm. Among other famous and first-class multipliers the Penn series should also be mentioned. These too are fairly expensive.

Sea miscellany

Photo 1. 'Breakaway' beachcasting leads. Photo 2. This is how the legs of the 'Breakaway' come free when the angler strikes or pulls hard to free it. The weight of a lead should always be adapted to the strength of the current (and of course to the capacity of your rod). Nevertheless I often see anglers fishing from a boat with far too light a lead. Always carry several sizes of whatever sort of lead is required.
Photo 3. Various types of sea leads for boat fishing and for general beachcasting.
Photograph 4 deserves further comment. Night anglers, fishing from piers or groynes, usually lose a lot of lead – as do boat anglers fishing over snaggy bottoms – and, what is worse, lose quite a few fish, often very fine specimens. This may not be entirely unavoidable, but I frequently see anglers who fail to wind fast enough or lift their rods when bringing in their tackle or a fish near to rocks, or underwater obstacles near the groynes or piers. It may not always be possible to save the lead when it jams in between the stones, rocks or whatever, but many a fish could be saved if the angler only took the trouble to tie on a weaker length of line than his main line between his lead and the boom, rather than clipping it straight on. This is not a tip to use when long casting as the weaker line to the lead may well break dur-

ing a forceful cast, but for use when fishing close or from a boat.

Never walk between loose boulders in the water to recover a fish or a line. Covered in sharp little mussels they can damage both skin and clothing, and a foot could jamb between the boulders.

A word about artificial bait for sea fishing. I have had little success in south and east coast areas with 'pirks'. The water is probably too cloudy, but further south into Hampshire, Devon and Cornwall they are very good. Close to the beach flatfish may sometimes be caught with a baited spoon. Personally, I have only caught postage-stamp sized flounders, but others have fortunately had better results.

In addition there are all kinds of rubber or plastic artificial worms which I consider

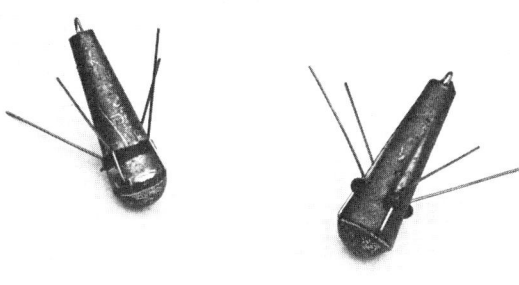

1

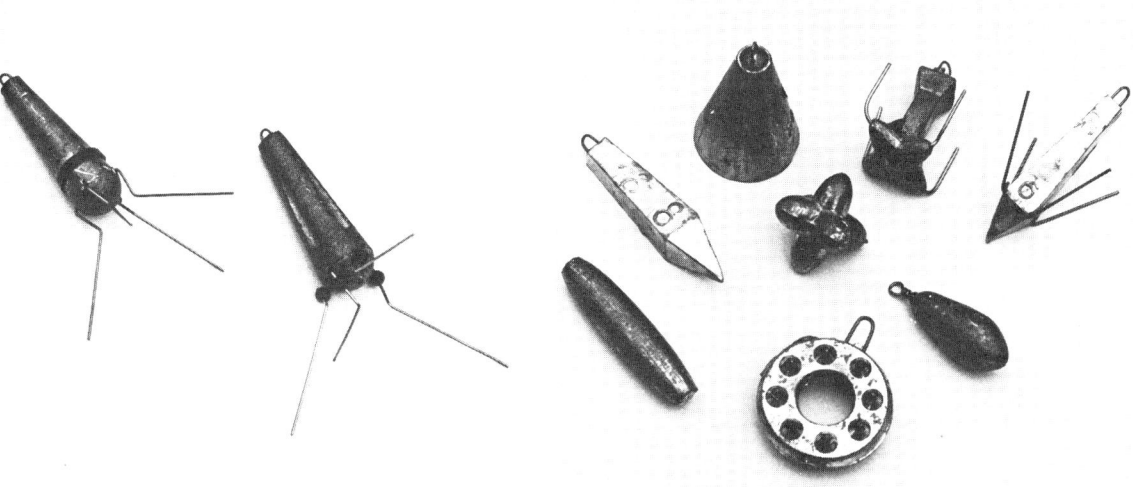

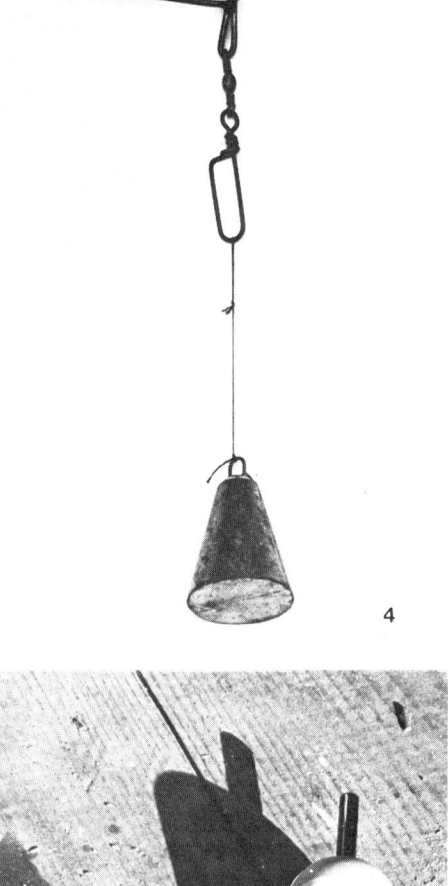

worthless. An old seal hunter I know once said to me: "These things catch fish all right – they'll laugh themselves to death and all you have to do is scoop them up."

4

Photo 5. Sea floats.
The size of float and buoyancy required is not always allied to the size of fish one hopes to catch, but often to the roughness of the sea. One may need a large buoyant float to remain on the surface during a heavy swell, or in rough rocky areas.

5

Photo 6. Various kinds of spoons and pirks for sea fishing, the latter intended mainly for cod. The triangular stave-shaped ones are the pirks.

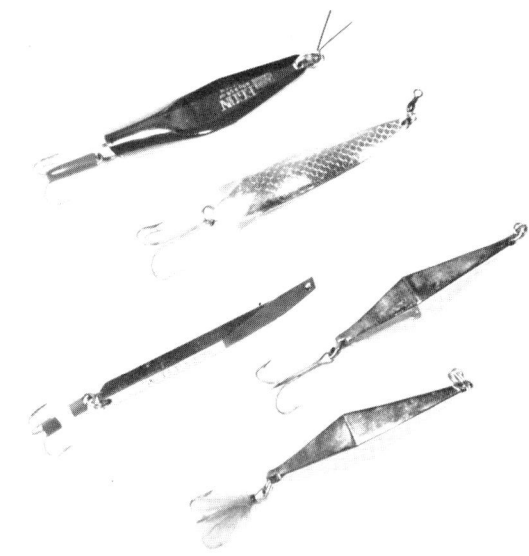

Photo 7. A plain spoon may be used as an attractor while the hook is baited with a lugworm or a ragworm. Because of the three-way swivel shown, the spoon blade in the centre turns freely in the current, so that, while the rod remains stationary, one is nevertheless fishing actively. I have caught a lot of whiting fishing in this manner, but several of my friends have taken bigger fish, namely excellent cod.

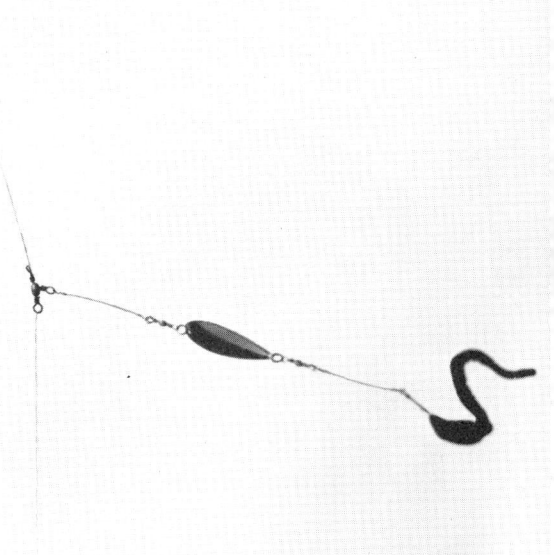

Photo 8. A simple but effective sea-rod rest. It consists of a good length of plastic tubing, cut obliquely at one end. Pushed into the beach, the lower end is filled with sand, keeping the rod perfectly stable.

Of course there are many other serviceable rod rests, but some of them have their drawbacks. To begin with, a spike, that screws into the lower end of a rod: in some cases it may be reversed for transport and storage. In strong winds I have seen the lower end of a rod split by this spike attachment. (By the way, unbreakable rods exist only in the imagination of their manufacturers.) Rod rests in which the rod is inserted are better, but in some places they cannot be fixed.

Photo 9. This practical weatherproof suit is particularly useful in winter. It is feather-light and is lined with glass fibre insulating material. The trousers have zip fasteners opening at either end, so that the boots need not be removed when the trousers are taken off. The jacket zip fastener also opens at either end, while the zipped pockets, including the inside one, are watertight. When the suit is completely fastened, the angler's face is protected to the chin. There are several makes on the market. Expensive, but essential for winter cod fishing.

Photo 10. In this photograph the line where current and counter-current meet is clearly visible. This is where a great deal of food sinks to the bottom and it is therefore a favourite feeding spot for sea fish. Moreover, a clear band of water occurs at this spot, and this is where bass, if it is present at all, may be found.

Photo 11. A good bag of flounders and a mullet. One can catch fish like these, and the occasional fair sized bass is also possible, in such a place as that shown in the previous photograph.

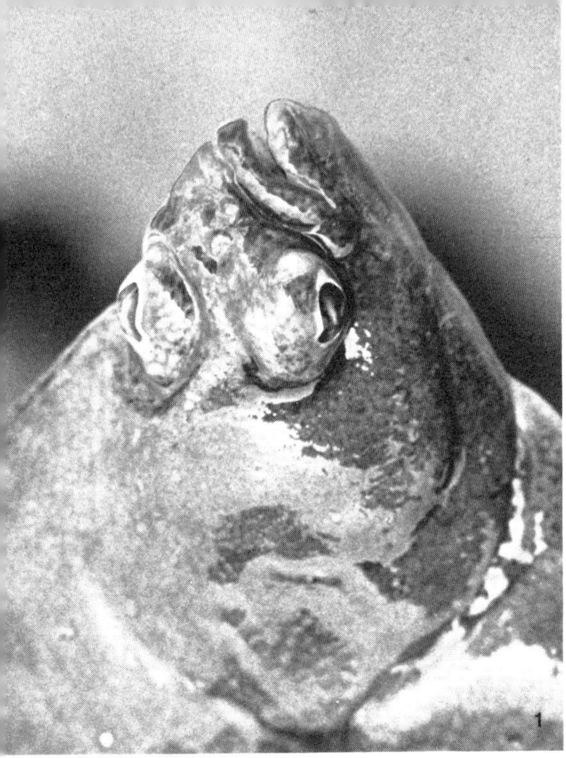

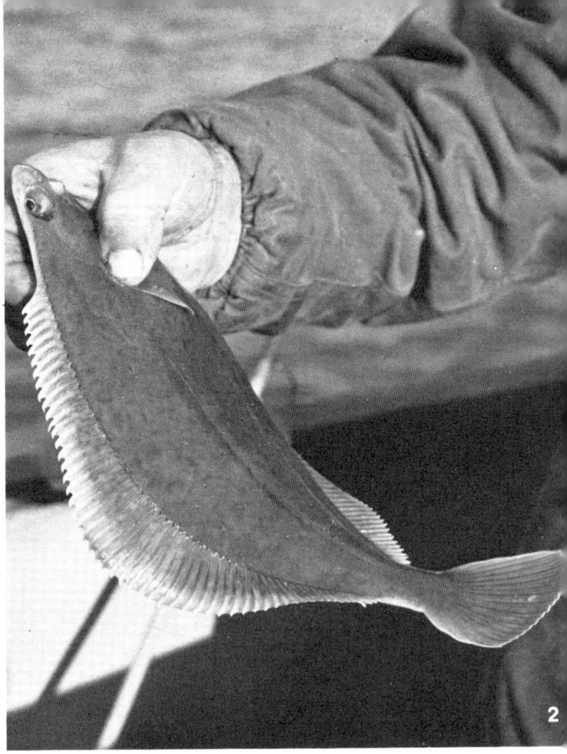

THE FISH

Flatfish

Apart from the mackerel, there is probably no fish so eagerly sought for eating as the various kinds of flatfish (flounder, plaice, and dab, to mention only those most frequently caught). Unfortunately the angling methods used for these fish are lacking in imagination and variety. I am guilty of this lack of experiment myself, but should like to tell you about a number of 'other' methods with which I have had results.

Appearance

Photograph 1 gives a good idea of a flatfish's characteristic face. When young a flatfish is shaped like other fish and swims in the same way. Later it changes: one eye moves round to join the other and the fish begins to swim on its side. In some species both eyes are placed on the right, in others on the left. The position of the mouth clearly shows the original shape of the fish. Its slant also indicates the advisability of using a slightly bent hook. It is often difficult to distinguish between flounder (photo 2) and plaice (photo 3), especially since there are many hybrids among flatfish. Flounder (*Platichtys flesus*) is best recognised by the easily felt bumps on its back (which is not really its back). Plaice (*Pleuronectes platessa*) is slightly broader and more lozenge-shaped: it is blotched with red and looks and feels smooth. Dab (*Limanda limanda*) (photo 4) is most easily recognised by its rough skin, like fine emery paper to the touch. Remember that

5

6

the minimum takeable size for dab is 15 cm. and for sole 24 cm. I shall say no more about the sole (*Solea solea*), recognised by its elongated oval shape and the fins extending along its entire body. Unfortunately this delicious fish is rarely caught with a rod these days. It is a night hunter. If your efforts are specially aimed at catching this fish, you should use a small hook, for instance an Aberdeen.

Little need be said about the most current (and well-known) angling method. A terminal lead is used with, as a rule, three hooklinks or a metal paternoster boom with longshank flounder hooks. Kirby hooks (with oblique point) not too large, are baited with lugworms or ragworms. Cast,

and wait until the rod tip indicates a bite. If dab are present this will happen continuously, for this fish is just as greedy as the mackerel. You are in that case unlikely to catch any other fish (in any case dab is very good to eat!). It occurs in summer until far into a mild autumn. Few plaice are caught from the shore: as a rule they are small. From a boat the catch will be better.

If the fish are biting well there are no problems, but if not, do try some experiments. Do not just fish passively, but after casting wait a few minutes, then draw the bait 1 to 2 yards towards you and repeat the process. When the fish are lazy this often has good results. Ragworm makes better bait than lugworm for this method (since it is

firmer), but I have also often been successful with a piece of fish on the hook. In any case you should always use different bait on the three hooks and observe whether fish are caught with the bottom hook only: in that case it is advisable to attach a good-sized lead above the leader (this may or may not be a sliding lead), so that all three hooks will lie on the bottom.

I should particularly like to draw your attention to angling with a baited spoon. I prefer a spoon with a round blade, but I have noticed excellent results with the double spoon shown in photograph 5 (p. 101). While I was fishing (unsuccessfully) for garfish on the outer side of a harbour wall, another angler, using this double

spoon, caught plenty of flounder close to the inner side, while the passive method of other fishermen was practically fruitless. At this point something should be said about baits for sea fishing. The ones most frequently used are ragworm (*Nereis pelagica*) and lugworm (*Arenicola piscatorum*). These may be dug up on the beach, but are for sale as well. They are becoming more and more expensive, but angling is in any case not such a cheap sport as it was.

Lugworm can be kept for a few days by individually rolling them in newspaper when they will 'dry out' and become very tough compared to the fresh 'watery' animal. For long casting the tougher bait has

103

obvious advantages and is well taken by cod or bass as well as flatfish. Some experienced anglers insert it on to a large Aberdeen hook *tail* first instead of the more usual head first.

Another useful bait is raw or cooked mussel. Raw is best: insert the hook through the foot (after removing the shell of course). This bait is very soft; it is more easily handled if it is boiled, removed from the shell and left in cold water for a couple of hours. This will make it much firmer. You may also be able to buy young herring. The hook should be passed through twice and if necessary the fish should be further secured with cotton thread. In the chapter on garfish, photographs 4–6 (pp. 118–19),

you will find further details on the use of fish as bait.

To revert to the sea bait in most current use: the ragworm (a 'sea centipede') can be cut up and hooked easily (see photos 7, 8, 9 and 10, pp. 102/3). If you are afraid of the tiny pinprick which the worm may give you with its head pinchers, you can use a pair of forceps.

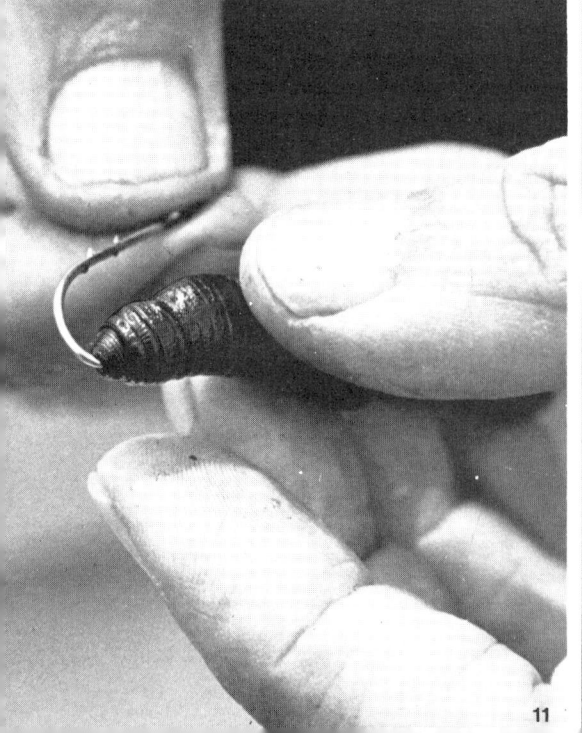

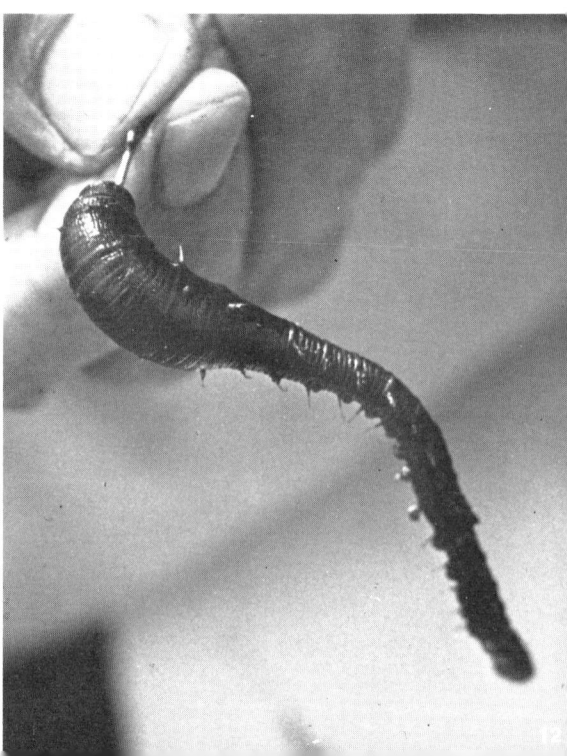

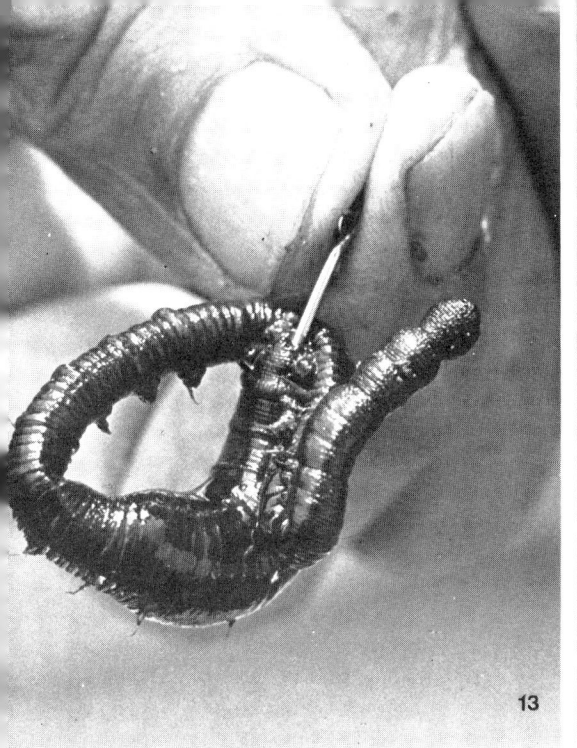

Photographs 11, 12 and 13 show the usual way in which a lugworm is hooked. Make sure that the point of the hook is inserted in the head opening, otherwise the worm will 'run out'. In photograph 14 you will see how the bait is presented.

Codling

Fishing for codling from a boat

In many respects it is easier to fish for codling (i.e. small cod) from a boat than from a pier, groyne or beach. Nevertheless, this method of angling presents its own problems.

To begin with, it is necessary to use the shorter rod – a boat rod – available in various lengths and price ranges. A long beach rod may be strained with heavy leads and one must be careful of one's fellow anglers. Reeling in the fish also creates a number of problems in a boat, especially when the angler's position vis-à-vis the water is rather high.

It should be mentioned here that on most boats equipment may be hired, but that as a rule this is of poor quality. Whenever possible bring your own sea reel loaded with 30 lb. line, or, if you have some experience and prefer a lighter line, at least 20 lb., with rod to match.

Bait, too, may sometimes be bought on board. Lugworms are excellent, but I still prefer ragworms (photo 1, opposite). Don't be mean when fishing for codling: it has a large mouth and likes a big snack, a few lugworms or a good-sized piece of ragworm. The hook I prefer is a large barbed shank hook, which holds the bait firmly and penetrates well. Pieces of fish, small herring, and mussels also make good bait.

Playing and landing big sea fish

Photograph 3 (opp.) shows the correct method of playing heavy fish. The angler in the picture is 'pumping', that is, he draws the fish towards himself by lifting the rod, without using the reel. He then winds down the line against nil pressure but keeping the line taught. This method was described in the section on carp fishing, pp. 57–58. Hoisting the fish by means of the reel (this applies to all heavy fish) is disastrous to expensive equipment. (See also the chapter on mackerel, pp. 112–15.) Although a multiplier will bear far more pressure it remains advisable in that case, too, to use the pumping method where big fish are concerned.

Bringing the fish inboard

You will usually not have caught sight of the fish during the struggle. As a rule, however, you know that it is a codling, or even a cod, because of its heavy thumping. Now the prisoner must be brought inboard. Merely hoisting it up on the line nearly always results in failure, not because the line will break, but because the fish's mouth will get torn. Any decent sea fishing boat will have at least one good gaff on board and there will always be willing hands to gaff the fish. Unfortunately this is often done very clumsily. Unlike, for instance, pike, cod must not be hooked in the gills, but in the stomach. The gaff is lowered under the fish when it is close to the boat: one should now strike without hesitation. Photographs 5 and 6 (p. 108) show how it is done, but I would prefer to keep the fish between gaff and boat and hook it from the far side.

Another way to bring the fish aboard is by means of a large rectangular or circular net with a strong cord. This is lowered by a fellow-angler. The angler drags the fish above the net, so that his colleague can bring it aboard. Such a net is shown in

107

5

6

photograph 9 (p. 110). It will be obvious to everyone that when landing a heavy fish (not only codling), a dropnet is no superfluous luxury.

In photograph 10 you see a lady with a codling caught while it was snowing.

Night fishing at sea is a very special experience and is, moreover, frequently very successful.

At those times when codling comes close to the shore, that is, in late autumn and frequently in winter, anglers will be found in large numbers along the coast and on breakwaters. This is an attractive sight, since each group has a strong lamp, for instance a Tilly lamp, or even a strong electric light run from a car battery. Caution on the

slippery stones is indicated, but it is certainly a grand adventure. It was on such an occasion that I caught the largest cod of my angling career, just over $19\frac{3}{4}$ lb.

Lighting creates a problem when you have a job to do with your hands. A 'miner's headlamp', or better still, illuminated spectacles, as illustrated in photograph 11 (p. 111), provide a solution. If you do not want to go to such expense, a slender pocket torch held between the teeth will serve. There is no doubt that catches made at night give extra pleasure (photo 12, p. 111).

Disgorging cod

Unlike pike, cod may be held by its mouth

while unhooking. Although this fish, too, has teeth, they are very tiny and harmless. Nevertheless I prefer to hold it by the gills (photo 7, below). Angler's forceps (see photo 8), artery forceps, or a pair of pincers are all very useful.

As a rule I avoid writing about the miraculous catches I have made, for even when true, few readers will believe me. However, I must describe an experience I once had when night fishing for codling — an experience which can be vouched for by two witnesses. It happened when fishing from the beach, where I had been standing with two angling friends since two in the afternoon without catching anything better than a few small flatfish. We had intended to go home early, but what would you do, if just before dusk codling made an appearance? One of us went to fetch a torch (it took an hour to the car and back), but it proved to give poor light. And then it happened. The tip of my rod curved in that beautiful gentle way which makes an angler's heart beat faster. And indeed, from the fish's thrashing I knew immediately that it was a big one. As we were fishing from the beach, it seemed a simple matter to land it. All I had to do was to walk backwards, winding in a little at intervals. Then the codling (which later proved to be worthy of the name 'cod') arrived in shallow water and my two friends went out to meet it and help it on its way. Believe it or not, one

7

8

of them stepped on the line (14 lb. – I find that heavy enough when fishing from the beach). Filled with despair I felt the line collapse: broken! I will spare you the language I uttered at that moment. But St. Peter was merciful. The fish was so close that my friends managed to bring it in. It weighed $19\frac{3}{4}$ lb. There is a moral to this story. The man who had broken my line contritely carried my catch to the car, but just before we left he himself had an equally good bite. When he wound in, his line broke. This really was carrying justice too far . . .

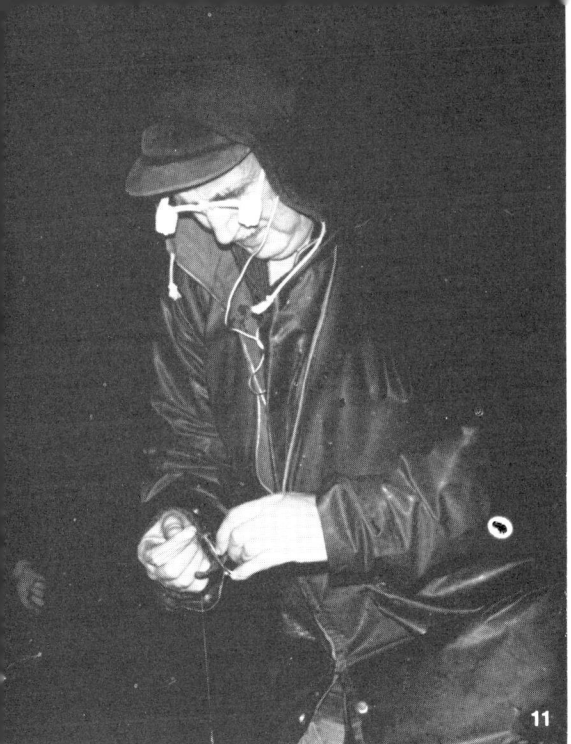

Photo 9. A round net suitable for scooping up a large fish.

Photo 10. Codling caught with rod and line from a boat.

Photo 11. Illuminated spectacles can be useful for night fishing.

Photo 12. An element of surprise — a large night-time catch.

Mackerel and scad

"There's mackerel about!" When this cry is heard – and it's quite remarkable how quickly such a report does the rounds in the anglers' world – angling fever reaches its height, for when there is mackerel off the shore (not just the odd one which has lost its way, but entire shoals) any green-horn will be able to catch them, and by several methods. I shall therefore devote a little extra attention to this stripy hunter. However, a shoal rarely consists of mackerel only, as a rule it is accompanied by another species, the scad or horse mackerel, so the latter will be discussed as well.

Appearance

Photograph 8 (p. 115) clearly shows the difference between the horse mackerel (*Trachurus trachurus*) (left) and the mackerel (*Scomber scombrus*) (right). Horse mackerel is smaller than mackerel (12 inches as against 20 inches): it lacks the latter's beautiful back marking, but has a viciously sharp dorsal fin and prickly scales along the lateral line. It does not have a very good name among fishermen and as a rule the angler is advised to throw the fish back, as being uneatable. I don't agree: even though the flesh is rather coarser and the fish possibly has more bones, it is reasonably good to eat.

Mackerel and scad have the same mode of

life. They lack an air-bladder and are therefore able to change depth rapidly. They hunt by sight and must keep on swimming to survive. Most publications on the subject will tell you that they usually hunt at high levels, but I know from recent experience that they sometimes seek a living at great depths.

Mackerel occurs along our coasts from April until well into summer: horse mackerel appears a little earlier.

Too easily caught to be amusing

Mackerel fishing provides a further proof of something that every true angler will have experienced: if large quantities of one species of fish are caught too easily and without variation in the method used, one soon gets bored. All the same – and especially to a beginner – it is quite an experience to catch a hundred or so mackerel in one day of boat-fishing. The method could not be simpler: the angler uses a 'set of feathers', consisting of a number (often as many as six), of feathers of varying colours, each mounted on a single hook: the bottom is weighted with a sea lead. This gear is jigged up and down in the water, a fairly tiring operation. It is by no means exceptional that three or more mackerel will bite simultaneously. The following three tips may be useful:

1. Don't use six hooks, but at the most three. When winding in try to observe at

what depth the mackerel are swimming, so that you won't have to search the water at every level time and again.

2. When you have a bite on every hook, do not pull up, but start 'pumping', as described on p. 107. Your reel is not a hoist. Soon after the mackerel season dozens of damaged reels are brought to tackle shops for repair.

3. After you have caught sufficient mackerel for your own needs, you would do better to change your method. You could, for instance, try a spoon on a light spinning rod. True, you will 'only' catch one mackerel at a time, but in the first place these are frequently much finer specimens, and in the second place such a fish provides better sport than the poor wretches dangling from the feathers, trying to escape in every direction, so that all you pull up is a dead weight.

·The photographs speak for themselves, nevertheless a brief comment. The angler in photograph 1 is using a strong glass rod of medium length. He therefore has no trouble in winding in the two mackerel (photo 2), although the lower one is still putting up resistance. Photographs 4 and 5 show the correct method of unhooking: the angler holds the mackerel with the stomach facing the other way. This is because, just like some other sea fish, mackerel sometimes discharge a liquid with a disgusting smell: this is forcefully ejected

from the anus and causes stubborn stains. Photographs 6 and 7 show coloured and white feathers, as used on a paternoster. Photograph 8 has already been mentioned. And finally: don't worry if you should lose your last feather. A milk bottle top, pierced by the hook, or a piece of silver paper mounted in the same way, will make a good substitute. When they are hungry these greedy hunters will even take a bare hook.

7

8

Garfish

Appearance

No angler could possibly fail to recognise this fish. Garfish (*Belone belone*) is long (18–28 inches) and slender, with the body of an eel, the forked tail of a mackerel and a bill-shaped mouth, indicating that it is no vegetarian. Its entire structure points to the fact that this fish is a born hunter. In a fine spring it will make its appearance along the southern coasts as early as April: otherwise it arrives a little later. It hunts by sight and thus prefers clear water, often found where two currents meet and where sand and debris sink to the bottom. Garfish is moreover a surface feeder and hunts its prey at fairly high levels. It is sometimes caught near mackerel shoals. It's not a nice character: frequently it attacks fellow fish already hooked, biting holes in their bodies. Photograph 1 shows the fish's remarkable appearance: in photographs 2 and 3 you see the way in which *Belone belone* resists when hooked. It stands on its tail, cutting capers in all directions to get free. It cuts these capers even when at liberty and has thus acquired the reputation of an acrobat and a clown. For instance, it likes to jump over floating obstacles, betraying its presence to its own ultimate disaster, but to the angler's joy.

Garfish occurs in large shoals along the coast and when they are known to be present, anglers are seen standing shoulder to shoulder along harbour walls and piers. However, do not set your expectations too high. Both the author and the photographer of this book have often sought the fish in vain in places where large numbers had been caught the day before ... but where by then none was in sight, let alone caught. It is a capricious fish which appears and disappears with equal suddenness.

It would of course be easier to go after this fish in a boat, but here a difficulty arises. As already mentioned, garfish hunt close to the surface (in clear weather to about 12 feet) and must therefore be fished with floating bait. When fishing from a boat this would, in a current, create a disastrous entanglement of fine lines. In fact, it would be possible to cast a float only from the stern, or occasionally from the bow.

Methods

Though it may seem simple to enumerate the ways in which garfish can be caught, it must be said that there is very little in our beloved sport which may truly be called 'simple'. In view of the facts (a) that we want to fish from the shore, and (b) that garfish feeds close to the surface, it is obvious that long-distance casts, made with a minimum of noise, are most advantageous. I would therefore recommend a good long, soft rod and, especially, not too heavy a line (4 to 6 lb. breaking strain).

There are many kinds of garfish floats, but personally I much prefer a slim type that will carry half to an ounce of lead which is sometimes necessary to cast a long way. A friend of mine recommends that the top of a float should be painted black, but here I must disagree. A black float is easily seen from a boat, but this is not the case from the shore when the water is rough. When fishing from the shore you should therefore paint it red.

Garfish has hard, small jaws, and it is there-

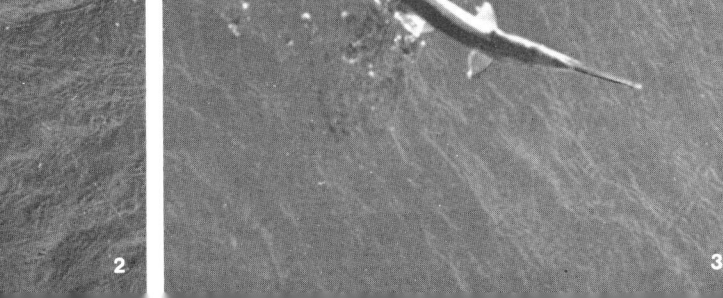

4

5

fore essential to use a sharp hook which holds the bait firmly. A 'Baitholder' hook no. 6 has been found excellent for the purpose.

Any sea bait is suitable, but best of all is a piece of fish, cut from the tail of a garfish, or if necessary from a mackerel. The way in which this is done is seen in photographs 4 and 5. With a razorblade (the back covered with Elastoplast) you cut an elongated triangle from the tail, leaving the flesh on the broad end, but cutting it away towards the point, thus making a fluttering little pennant. The hook is inserted through the thick end.

The bite
Though a fierce hunter, garfish is often very cautious. Before biting it has a good look at the proffered snack : this can be deduced from the eddy behind the float. A moment later the float disappears and as soon as this is definite, you should strike hard. Now begins a struggle which frequently ends in victory for the fish. Once you have caught it, remember to hold its stomach away from you, for it ejects an even more obnoxious mess than does the mackerel. It is advisable to scale and clean the fish immediately : because of its peculiar smell you should use a disposable cloth. It should be

mentioned that garfish is very good eating and that the green bones contain no harmful substance.

The last photograph in the book shows a lady with a large garfish — a yard of 'gar'.